Older and Stronger

Spiritual Nourishment for Aging Christians

Dora Isaac Weithers

TEACH Services, Inc.
P U B L I S H I N G
www.TEACHServices.com • (800) 367-1844

World rights reserved. This book or any portion thereof may not be copied or reproduced in any form or manner whatever, except as provided by law, without the written permission of the publisher, except by a reviewer who may quote brief passages in a review.

The author assumes full responsibility for the accuracy of all facts and quotations as cited in this book. The opinions expressed in this book are the author's personal views and interpretations, and do not necessarily reflect those of the publisher.

This book is provided with the understanding that the publisher is not engaged in giving spiritual, legal, medical, or other professional advice. If authoritative advice is needed, the reader should seek the counsel of a competent professional.

Copyright © 2022 Dora Isaac Weithers
Copyright © 2022 TEACH Services, Inc.
ISBN-13: 978-1-4796-1512-4 (Paperback)
ISBN-13: 978-1-4796-1513-1 (ePub)
Library of Congress Control Number: 2022915729

All Scripture Quotations, unless otherwise indicated, are taken from the Holy Bible, Easy-to-Read Version (ERV), Copyright © 2006 by Bible League International.

All Scripture references marked (AMP) are taken from the Amplified Bible, copyright © 2015 by The Lockman Foundation, La Habra, CA 90631. All rights reserved.

All Scripture references marked (CEV) are taken from the Contemporary English Version of the Bible, copyright © 1995 by American Bible Society.

All Scripture references marked (KJV) are taken from the King James Version of the Bible. Public domain.

All Scripture references marked (TLB) are taken from the Living Bible, copyright © 1971 by Tyndale House Foundation. Used by permission of Tyndale House Publishers Inc., Carol Stream, Illinois 60188. All rights reserved.

All Scripture references marked (MSG) are taken from The Message version of the Bible, copyright © 1993, 2002, 2018 by Eugene H. Peterson.

All Scripture references marked (NIV) are taken from the Holy Bible, New International Version®, NIV®, copyright © 1973, 1978, 1984, 2011 by Biblica, Inc.®. Used by permission. All rights reserved worldwide.

All Scripture references marked (NKJV) are taken from the New King James Version® of the Bible, copyright © 1982 by Thomas Nelson. Used by permission. All rights reserved.

All Scripture references marked (NLT) are taken from the *Holy Bible*, New Living Translation, copyright © 1996, 2004, 2015 by Tyndale House Foundation. Used by permission of Tyndale House Publishers, Inc., Carol Stream, Illinois 60188. All rights reserved.

The author assumes full responsibility for the accuracy and interpretation of the Ellen White quotations cited in this book.

TEACH Services, Inc.
PUBLISHING
www.TEACHServices.com • (800) 367-1844

CONTENTS

Preface vi

Section One: Purpose 11

    Cupful #1— God Needs You   13
    Cupful #2—A Prayer for Purpose   16
    Cupful #3—Moving Forward   19
    Cupful #4—Helping Others   22
    Cupful #5—Helping with Words   25
    Cupful #6—Wholehearted Devotion   28
    Cupful #7—Serving with Humility   32
    Cupful #8—Does God Really Speak?   36
    Cupful #9—The Good Life   40
    Cupful #10—Unfading Beauty   43
    Cupful #11—Testimonies   47
    Cupful #12—Embracing Change   50
    Cupful #13—The Joy of Obedience   53
    A Seventeenth-Century Nun's Prayer   56

Section Two: Faith 59

    Cupful #14—Stronger Faith   61
    Cupful #15—Contentment   64
    Cupful #16—Faithfulness in Older Men   67
    Cupful #17—Goodness in Older Women   70
    Cupful #18—God Can Do Anything   73
    Cupful #19—A Prayer for Joy   76

Cupful #20—Loving and Forgiving	79
Cupful #21—Don't Be Afraid	82
Cupful #22—Worship Responses	85
Cupful #23—God's Intervention	89
Cupful #24—Hold Me	92
Cupful #25—The Living Sermon	95
Cupful #26—Harvest Time	98
"Leave It There" by Charles A. Tindley	101

Section Three: Hope 103

Cupful #27—More and More Hope	105
Cupful #28—The Purpose of the Wind	109
Cupful #29—Be Brave	112
Cupful #30—Money	116
Cupful #31—Be Ready Always	119
Cupful #32—The Death of Saints	122
Cupful #33—God's Smile	125
Cupful #34—When You Need Help	128
Cupful #35—A Legacy of Kindness	131
Cupful #36—God's Expectations	134
Cupful #37—Teaching by Example	137
Cupful #38—A Prayer for Wisdom	140
Cupful #39—A Good Future	143
"Jesus Loves Me, This I Know" (Senior Version, author unknown)	146

Section Four: Love 149

Cupful #40—More and More Love	151
Cupful #41—Forgive and Remember	154
Cupful #42—Be Happy	157
Cupful #43—A Prayer for Loved Ones	160
Cupful #44—Bruised but Not Destroyed	163

Contents

Cupful #45—Things We Remember	166
Cupful #46—Love Is Patient	169
Cupful #47—The Beauty of Kindness	172
Cupful #48—Fellowship with God	175
Cupful #49—The Searching Shepherd	178
Cupful #50—Sabbath Rest	181
Cupful #51—Christmas Celebration	184
Cupful #52—Reserved Blessings	187
"Fruitfulness in Old Age"	190

PREFACE

The story of Elizabeth in the New Testament gives us hope that some of the blessings we did not receive in our prime years will be delivered in our senior years. Elizabeth prayed for a child—prayed, trusted, and maintained her faith, even when it seemed that her prayer had expired.

No presumptuous action by Elizabeth, unlike Sarah, who thought that time was running out on God.

No unreasonable demand on her husband, unlike Rachel, who seemed to think that the man could manipulate the woman's womb.

No whining about diminished womanhood, although she thought, like Hannah, that womanhood without motherhood lacks value.

Elizabeth prayed and continued living a life surrendered to God. She and her priestly husband, Zechariah, maintained their commitment and "did everything the Lord commanded, always following his instructions completely" (Luke 1:6). In God's own time, the angel Gabriel appeared to Zechariah with the news: "Your prayer has been heard by God. Your wife Elizabeth will give birth to a baby boy" (Luke 1:13). The angel used her story to prove to the Virgin Mary, and to all of us, that God answers prayers according to His schedule (see Luke 1:26–37).

What if God has waited to deliver in our senior years, some of the answers for which we prayed two or three decades ago? What if He is granting us some bonus years to fulfill a neglected dream that He put within us when we

Preface

were younger? What if He has delayed a blessing in order to have our children and grandchildren witness it, so that they could imitate the faith and trust they see in us?

Older and Stronger aims to convince us that God has a purpose for having us live as long as we have. Whatever the reason, we do well to show our gratitude by embracing Him in complete surrender. He has promised that He will never leave nor forsake us (see Deut. 31:6), and that while we abide in Christ, He has work for us to do (see Eph. 2:10).

Even when our bodies begin to show decline, His Spirit will strengthen our spirits. "That is why we never give up. Our physical body is becoming older and weaker, but our spirit inside us is made new every day" (2 Cor. 4:16).

Older and Stronger was written to help us fortify the strength of "our spirit inside us." We will learn that as long as we are alive and able, God helps us to improve our character, to flourish and be productive in ways that glorify Him, in ways that extend His Kingdom. In the process, we become stronger in purpose and in the graces that last forever—faith, hope, and love (1 Cor. 13:13).

So, for those who are ready to grow stronger in spirit while the body ages, join us in a weekly devotion (each one, a cupful of spiritual nutriment) which has been specially prepared for individuals in or near their senior years. There are fifty-two presentations, one for each week of the year, but not dated, so you may begin at any time, with any cupful. Each week, there is one scriptural capsule, fortified with nutrients to provide spiritual, mental, and emotional strength.

Take one cupful on Sunday and experience the boost again as often as you like during the week. There is also a quotation for Sunday, which aims to add depth to your meditation. From Monday to Saturday, the accompanying prayer guide will help you focus on personal application.

Enjoy each cupful of nutriment by yourself, or enjoy it even more with a spouse, friend, caregiver, or anyone who wishes to participate. The devotionals and prayer guide may benefit an entire prayer team.

Spending time with God and His Word every day adds joy and meaning to life. He will empower you to become

> the lovable older person folks like to be around;
> the model of joy, hope, and courage to those who are afraid to grow old;
> the display of God's favor on those whom He makes older and stronger.

Celebrate the strength that God has given you to be productive in your later years. It is your time to testify

> that He is good;
> that He forgives the misdeeds of your past;
> that you appreciate the opportunity in your bonus years to represent Him better than you have ever done.

Enjoy growing older and stronger by His grace!

Never Grow Old

By James C. Moore

> I have heard of a land
> On the faraway strand,
> 'Tis a beautiful home of the soul;
> Built by Jesus on high,
> There we never shall die,
> 'Tis a land where we never grow old.

Refrain:
Never grow old,
Where we'll never grow old,
In a land where we'll never grow old;
Never grow old,
Where we'll never grow old,
In a land where we'll never grow old.

In that beautiful home
Where we'll nevermore roam,
We shall be in the sweet by and by;
Happy praise to the King
Through eternity sing,
'Tis a land where we never shall die. [Refrain]

When our work here is done
And the life crown is won,
And our troubles and trials are o'er,
All our sorrows will end,
And our voices will blend
With the loved ones who've gone on before. [Refrain]

Seven Bible Promises for Older Folk

1. My soul, praise the LORD! Every part of me, praise his holy name! ... He gives us plenty of good things. He makes us young again, like an eagle that grows new feathers. (Ps. 103:1, 5)
2. The righteous will flourish like a palm tree, they will grow like a cedar of Lebanon; planted in the house of the LORD, they will flourish in the courts of our God. They will still bear fruit in old age, they will stay fresh and green, proclaiming, "The Lord is upright." (Ps. 92:12–15, NIV)

3. I have carried you since you left your mother's womb. I carried you when you were born, and I will still be carrying you when you are old. Your hair will turn gray, and I will still carry you. I made you, and I will carry you to safety. (Isa. 46:3–4)
4. I was young and now I am old, yet I have never seen the righteous forsaken or their children begging bread. (Ps. 37:25, NIV)
5. That is why we never give up. Our physical body is becoming older and weaker, but our spirit inside us is made new every day. (2 Cor. 4:16)
6. Maybe my mind and body will become weak, but God is my source of strength. He is mine forever! (Ps. 73:26)
7. When my followers call to me, I will answer them. I will be with them when they are in trouble. I will rescue them and honor them. I will give my followers a long life and show them my power to save. (Ps. 91:15–16)

SECTION ONE
Purpose

"The purpose of whatever you do should be to help everyone grow stronger in faith."

(1 Corinthians 14:26)

"God created you with a definite purpose in mind. Your existence is evidence that this generation needs something that your life contains."

"You are designed for your purpose. You are perfect for your purpose."

"Success is obedience to purpose."

(Munroe, 1992)

CUPFUL #1

GOD NEEDS YOU

The Lord wants to use you for special purposes.
(2 Timothy 2:21)

At about the age of eight, it dawned on me that folks might consider my grandmother illiterate. She never carried a Bible or hymnal to church, yet she sang most of the songs and recited much of the scripture reading.

"Mamma, don't you care if people think that you can't read?" I queried.

"It doesn't matter," she stated with confidence. "Some members really can't read, and when they see me singing without a book, they might try to do the same."

My grandmother's eyesight had been deteriorating, and by the time we had this conversation, she could read only large billboards. Instead of grieving at what she had lost, she chose to influence others with what she still had—*strength of mind* to recall song lyrics and scriptures, *strength of spirit* to worship with confidence despite her poor vision, and *strength of character* to remain true to her purpose rather than waste time proving that she could read.

Your purpose in your old age is determined by the skills and abilities you still have. No matter your method—

Older and Stronger

story telling, encouragement, singing, mentoring, gardening, praying—your contribution counts. God is giving you the opportunity to give back some of what you have been given. You live to enrich the lives of others and to build your own legacy. You live to use the spiritual gifts God has given you for your special assignments. By using your gifts consistently, you strengthen your purpose. Stay ready for Him to use. He needs you!

> Instead of grieving at what she had lost, she chose to influence others with what she still had—*strength of mind* to recall song lyrics and scriptures, *strength of spirit* to worship with confidence despite her poor vision, and *strength of character* to remain true to her purpose rather than waste time proving that she could read.

PRAYER: Heavenly Father, please show us how to use every bit of our lives, every skill and talent we still have, for Your glory. In Jesus' name, Amen.

This Week's Prayer Guide

Sunday
"If God only used perfect people, nothing would get done. God will use anybody if you're available" (Rick Warren).

Monday
Read 1 Timothy 2:21: "The Lord wants to use you for special purposes, so make yourself clean from all evil. Then you will be holy, and the Master can use you. You will be ready for any good work." Pray and believe that God will cleanse you so that He can use you. Give Him thanks and pray for cleansing as often as you feel the need.

Tuesday

Think of one special purpose for which God used you in the past. Did you feel happy? Blessed? Grateful? Thank Him and ask Him for more opportunities to be used again.

Wednesday

Instead of "you will be holy," as it says in our focus verse, other versions say that you will be a "vessel of honor." This is a title of worth. Claim this title for yourself, and thank God for placing His kingdom value on you.

Thursday

If you know the song "Take My Life and Let It Be" written by Frances Ridley Havergal, sing it prayerfully. Or just meditate on the words:

> Take my life and let it be consecrated, Lord, to thee.
> Take my moments and my days;
> let them flow in endless praise,
> let them flow in endless praise.

Friday

Pray to be always available and humble when God chooses a specific work for you to do. Pray for obedience and courage to perform your assignment. Get your blessing!

Saturday

Pray to remain in fellowship with God, for Him to nurture your strength and empower your skills, to be always useful to Him.

CUPFUL #2

A PRAYER FOR PURPOSE

> Now that I am old and my hair is gray, don't leave me, God. I must tell the next generation about your power and greatness.
>
> (PSALM 71:18)

This verse is appropriate for every aging person to pray. Entire churches can pray this prayer for their seniors. It enhances old age with privilege and purpose.

"Don't leave me" is not a request for God to wait while the individual catches up to Him as He is walking ahead. It is the desire of one who has been consistently close to Him, and who never wants to be separated.

This prayer conjures up the image of an older person clinging to God's strong arm, as he prepares for the natural forces which threaten his age group. He has watched some older folk become overwhelmed by physical and mental illnesses. He witnessed their loneliness as their colleagues passed on. Some reached out to him when their vision grew dim and their hearing diminished. Should he face any of these challenges, he wants them to find him cuddling with God.

The psalmist's desire for closeness is not for himself only. He remembers his children, his neighbor's children, and his friends' children, of whose world he is a part, and he wants the opportunity to tell them how great and how good God is. He wants to encourage them to lead godly lives, and to persevere in life's journey through their valleys and storms. He wants to tell them how he survived because of God's faithfulness. He wants to watch them surrender to God.

Has God laid on your heart a young person with whom to share your life's lessons? Share your testimony about the privilege of knowing Jesus as Savior and Lord. Tell how in fellowship with God, you surmounted obstacles, which you could have done only in His strength. Fulfill your purpose while you enjoy the privilege of being used by God.

PRAYER: Thank You, gracious God, for the purpose of representing You to the next generation. Help me to do it gladly. In Jesus' name, Amen.

This Week's Prayer Guide

Sunday
"Let us never know what old age is. Let us know the happiness time brings, not count the years" *(Ausonius)*.

Monday
As you age, in what areas of your life do you feel the greater need for God? Physical? Spiritual? Social? Emotional? Financial? Mention the details in your prayer, and trust God to do what's best for you.

Tuesday
Telling the next generation about God's power and greatness is one of the special purposes He has for you. Who is the first

on your list to tell? How do you intend to tell? By phone? Face to face? Letter or text message? Pray for the courage to fulfill your intentions.

Wednesday
Who introduced you to Christ? If you can, say thanks to that person. If it is not possible, thank God anyway, and ask God to bless your efforts the way He blessed the effort of the person who told you about Him.

Thursday
Pray to maintain a cheerful, not grumpy, attitude so that folks may enjoy your company and want to hear your stories. Also pray for patience and attentiveness to listen to the stories of others.

Friday
Sing or meditate on the words of "I'll Tell the World" by Baynard Fox:

> I'll tell the world, that I'm a Christian,
> I'm not ashamed, His name to bear;
> I'll tell the world, that I'm a Christian,
> I'll take Him with me anywhere.

Saturday
Psalm 71:18, our Scripture verse, is an appropriate prayer for every older Christian. Pray it today, and often.

CUPFUL #3

MOVING FORWARD

> I forget what is in the past and try as hard as I can to reach the goal before me.
>
> (PHILIPPIANS 3:13)

There are happy episodes from my past that come to mind occasionally. But if I think about them long enough, I may also remember some things I regret.

I like to remember my happy childhood. My cousins and I played outdoor games after school with our friends. We walked to the beach and picked seaside grapes. We laughed out loud when the stories were funny, and huddled together if they were scary. But I regret that all the cousins did not stay in touch.

I remember some special friendships and some pleasant conversations that still make me smile. But I also remember some breakups. There are many good times and good things in our past, which make us happy to recall them, but some of the joys have faded. Our present goal is satisfaction that lasts.

God's gift of salvation, through the death and resurrection of Jesus Christ, has granted us an opportunity for a better life—eternal life. The earthly joys we experienced in relationships, the great successes we achieved, and the lavish possessions we obtained were all means to an end.

They cannot compare with the glories of heaven.

There were regrets, too, and disappointments and failures. We cannot afford to waste our mental energy dwelling on them. We need that energy to help us move forward. Let us focus on where we are heading rather than on where we have been. What we are hoping for is more satisfying than what we have had. We're moving forward toward Heaven and eternal life with Jesus—forever.

> **Let us focus on where we are heading rather than on where we have been.**

PRAYER: Thank You, heavenly Father, for the eternal joys that await us in our eternal future. May nothing earthly hold us back. In Jesus' name, Amen.

This Week's Prayer Guide

Sunday
"The righteous shall move onward and forward; those with pure hearts shall become stronger and stronger" (Job 17:9, TLB).

Monday
The Apostle Paul continued in Philippians 3 verses 7–9, "At one time all these things [ancestry and accomplishments] were important to me… All I want now is Christ. I want to belong to him." (brackets added) What good things are you willing to give up so that they do not prevent you from moving forward with Christ? Surrender them in prayer.

Tuesday
What negative things in your life (losses, accidents) prevent you from focusing on moving forward? Pray that God gives

you the grace to forgive the people you may have blamed. Accept God's forgiveness.

Wednesday
Sing or meditate on these words of "I'm Pressing on the Upward Way" by Johnson Oatman, Jr.:

> I'm pressing on the upward way, new heights I'm gaining every day;
> Still praying as I'm onward bound,
> "Lord, plant my feet on higher ground."
>
> My heart has no desire to stay where doubts arise and fears dismay;
> Though some may dwell where those abound,
> My prayer, my aim, is higher ground.

Thursday
Paul also says in verses 13 and 14, "I still have a long way to go ... I keep running hard toward the finish line." Pray for the strength to persevere 'til the end.

Friday
Is there someone you would like to have moving forward with you? Pray that God gives you success in recruiting him or her.

Saturday
Our final goal in moving forward is Heaven with Jesus. Pray to remain focused.

CUPFUL #4

HELPING OTHERS

> Then God has given a place to ... those who can help others.
>
> (1 Corinthians 12:29)

My retired-teacher friend recognizes that God has selected her to help others, and she is serious about performing her God-given assignments. Whenever she has the opportunity to help, she offers her service with the understanding that God expects her to do what He has given her the ability to do. She is driven not by the prospect of recognition and reward, but by her passion to improve the lives of needy persons whom God puts in her path.

She has been especially effective in helping struggling readers. One of her favorite stories is about a child who had such a poor educational start that he had to repeat kindergarten. My friend helped him deal with the self-doubt and insecurities that plagued his young life. She motivated him to make the effort necessary for his progress, and she reaped the joy and satisfaction of watching him advance to the second position in his class, all the way up to high school.

Perhaps in your later years, God is assigning you to become a helper in an area where you were once a leader. He expects you to function with all the capabilities you have, no matter

Helping Others

the role He selects for you. He is as much God when He helps as when He leads. And you are as faithful when you obey His call to help, as when you obey His call to lead.

One form of help that many people need is the help to accept Christ as their Savior. They have heard about God's love, but they need encouragement to let Jesus into their hearts and surrender to His guidance. They need to hear again about the peace and joy that come with confessing their sins and giving their hearts to Him in exchange for a new lifestyle. They may also need counsel to help with other challenges they face.

In gratitude for our lives and our God-given abilities, let us look all around us for opportunities to help those in need. What a privilege to be assigned by God to help someone!

PRAYER: Heavenly Father, we thank You for including us in Your salvation plan. Please use us to help in whatever way You ask. In Jesus' name, Amen.

This Week's Prayer Guide

Sunday
"Spectators sit and watch, but we are called to use our spiritual gifts and serve continually" (Charles Stanley).

Monday
In what areas do people often ask for your help? It is God who assigns you to give that kind of help. Thank Him for the opportunity to carry out His assignments. Ask Him for the strength to do the best you can.

Tuesday
Hebrews 6:10 says, "God is fair, and he will remember all the work you have done." What kind of reward do you expect

from Him? List one way in which you have been rewarded so far. Thank Him.

Wednesday
Hebrews 6:10 continues, "He will remember that you showed your love to him by helping his people." Pray to show love to God by helping, whomever and whenever you can.

Thursday
What will you say to a friend who tells you, "Nobody needs my help anymore. I'm too old."? Practice your response. Pray for the courage to speak it to someone who needs to hear it.

Friday
Do you ever refuse help even though you need it? Please realize that just as God has given you the opportunity to help others, He has also given others the opportunity to help you. Pray for humility to ask for and accept help when you need it.

Saturday
The nineteenth-century poet Emily Dickinson describes different ways to help. Add other ways in your prayer:

> If I can stop one heart from breaking,
> I shall not live in vain;
> If I can ease one life the aching,
> Or cool one pain,
> Or help one fainting robin
> Unto his nest again,
> I shall not live in vain.

CUPFUL #5

HELPING WITH WORDS

Say the right thing at the right time and help others by what you say.

(EPHESIANS 4:29, CEV)

The soloist was scheduled to sing on a Christian television program. She arrived guilt-ridden and looking downcast because of a wrong deed she had committed. Even though she had prayed about it, she did not feel forgiven. By divine appointment, a gentleman she had never met walked by, smiled, and said, "Don't look so scared; God already fixed it." Much better than a mere hello, the right words at the right time inspired her confidence. She manifested joy as she ministered in song.

When we take our Christian responsibility seriously, God will inspire us to say something good, which is also helpful. We are called to communicate to each other the words that we need in order to brighten our day, to remind us of our God-given worth, to strengthen our determination toward our God-given goals, to enliven our joy. Let us think of the purpose for the words we say, whether we are bosses or employees, teachers or students, caregivers or those receiving care.

When someone feels deprived or helpless, it may take the gracious words of another person to point out God's favor. That's by God's design. The attitude of both speaker and listener improves when we build each other up with the right words at the right time.

Say to the hard worker, "You're doing a good job." Tell the underprivileged, "What I've seen God do for others, I know that He can do for you." To the helpless, confused, or disappointed ask, "How can I help?" When such words come from our lips, our inner strength increases. Good words make us feel good, and helpful words move us forward.

When we are unable to help in any other way, God can still use us to build each other up with helpful words. God delights in speaking through us.

> Most of our unkind words are spoken to those who are closest to us—our family members. Pray for the patience to speak kindly to them.

> When we are unable to help in any other way, God can still use us to build each other up with helpful words.

PRAYER: Heavenly Father, we pray with thanksgiving that You will help us to help others with our words, the way You help us when we read or hear Your words. In Jesus' name, Amen.

This Week's Prayer Guide

Sunday
"Kind words can be short and easy to speak, but their echoes are truly endless" (Mother Teresa).

Monday
"So you must stop telling lies. 'You must always speak the truth to each other'" (Eph. 4:25). Pray to speak honestly, no matter what.

Tuesday
"Say … whatever will help them grow stronger. Then what you say will be a blessing to those who hear you" (verse 29). Pray for the grace and wisdom to speak blessings and encouragement to others.

Wednesday
"Don't make the Holy Spirit sad… Never be bitter, angry, or mad. Never shout angrily or say things to hurt others" (verses 30–31). Pray that you allow the Holy Spirit to control you and your temper.

Thursday
"Be kind and loving to each other. Forgive each other the same as God forgave you through Christ" (verse 32). Most of our unkind words are spoken to those who are closest to us—our family members. Pray for the patience to speak kindly to them.

Friday
Sing or meditate on these words of a prayer song "If Any Little Word of Mine" by F. E. Belden. They correspond with Paul's advice:

> If any little word of mine may make a dark life brighter,
> If any little song of mine may make a sad heart lighter,
> God help me speak the helping word,
> And sweeten it with singing.
> And drop it in some lonely vale,
> To set the echoes ringing.

Saturday
Reread the advice in the verses you read on Monday through Thursday. Pray to speak helpful, encouraging words to yourself, also.

CUPFUL #6

WHOLEHEARTED DEVOTION

> She was now very old... Anna was always at the Temple; she never left. She worshiped God by fasting and praying day and night.
>
> (LUKE 2:37)

After seven years of marriage, Anna (also called Hannah) became a widow. She spent all the years of her widowhood in wholehearted devotion. No crying over the pleasures she missed or the children she might have had. Instead, she chose to consecrate her total self to service for God. She was now 84 years old.

She participated in all the temple services. In private, she continued in prayer and fasting. Such a life would be challenging for young wives and mothers, but not as difficult for older widows, widowers, and other seniors. Anna demonstrated one way in which their lives can be purposeful.

When the eight-day-old Jesus was presented in the Temple, Anna discerned who the child really was. Other religionists saw just another baby, but Anna, who was focused on matters of spiritual significance, recognized the Messiah. She was the first woman to give testimony of Jesus, the Christ. She "spoke of Him to all those who looked for redemption" (Luke 2:38, NKJV).

Older Christian men and women whose lives are centered on prayer and devotion can become ministry assets. No time for criticism of the church ministers or programs, no time for gossip about the sins of other congregants, no time to complain about their own mistakes and pet peeves. They share a prayer and a word from God, which they receive in their intimate conversations with Him.

Still wondering about your value as an older member in your congregation? With an attitude of wholehearted devotion like Anna's, you have time to pray for your salvation and intercede for the salvation of others. Other members are learning from you. God needs you and He honors your devotion!

PRAYER: Heavenly Father, please bless our devotion beyond our active years of service. We thank you for the extended privilege, in Jesus' name. Amen.

This Week's Prayer Guide

Sunday
"An aged Christian ... contented, thankful, grave, pious, and consistent—how becoming, how engaging, and how venerable!" (James Foote).

Monday
Before you pray to be wholeheartedly devoted, meditate on the second stanza of "Take Time to Be Holy," written by William D. Longstaff:

> Take time to be holy, the world rushes on;
> Spend much time in secret with Jesus alone.

By looking to Jesus like Him thou shalt be;
Thy friends in thy conduct His likeness shall see.

Tuesday
Do you crave more devotional time now that you're older? Pray that nothing will distract you from your daily devotional habit.

Wednesday
Fasting (eliminating or reducing the amount of food for a specific time period and purpose, often for prayer) is not compulsory, but consider the following:

Anna fasted as part of her worship. (Luke 2:37)
Jesus fasted in preparation for His life's mission. (Luke 4: 1–2)
(You may want to consult with your doctor before deciding to fast.)
Pray for God's guidance concerning fasting as a part of your worship.

Thursday
In a life of devotion is there any space for joy and laughter? Of course. The Holy Spirit produces joy (Gal. 5:22). God's goodness to you provides much to celebrate and laugh about. Recall some pleasurable moments God provided in the past, and thank Him.

Friday
Is there an older person whose example of continual devotion inspires you? Pray for that person. Pray that you also become an example to someone.

Saturday
Anna worshiped day and night. Pray for grace to maintain a regular worship schedule even if you are isolated during a pandemic.

CUPFUL #7

SERVING WITH HUMILITY

> Be fair to other people. Love kindness and loyalty,
> and humbly obey your God.
>
> (MICAH 6:8)

Mr. Breton reminds himself that he is not perfect, probably because many of his former students seem to think that he is. Now in his eighties, he is still privileged to receive visits from them. They bring their children to meet him.

Obviously, he taught more than academics. The young adults tell stories of his firm but caring discipline and his positive influence on the choices they made. Still, instead of settling into satisfaction about the success stories he hears, Mr. Breton leans heavily on the counsel in 1 Corinthians 10:12, "So anyone who thinks they are standing strong should be careful that they don't fall."

Mr. Breton wants humility to be part of the legacy he leaves behind. He gives credit to God for his ability to share knowledge, help, guidance, and any other good thing his protégés receive from him. Whenever he gets a chance, He

Serving with Humility

pushes God to the forefront. He presents himself as just a vessel, used by God.

One day, a technician installed an appliance in Mr. Breton's kitchen, and then informed him that he did not want to be paid. Mr. Breton did not even remember that he had taught the young man. The man said that were it not for the teacher's direction, he would not be fit for gainful employment. The teacher ascribed praise and gratitude to God for the young man's self-development and his positive contribution to society.

How do you tell the stories of your accomplishments? Do you give credit to God, and to the kindness and loyalty of other persons who helped you? Take a page from Mr. Breton's book. Acknowledge your success and remember to mention that it was God who won the victories on your behalf. Humility looks great on older people. Boast about God. He honors those who honor Him (see 1 Sam.2:30). That includes you.

> **Acknowledge your success and remember to mention that it was God who won the victories on your behalf.**

PRAYER: Gracious God, we give You all the power, and honor, and glory for all the good You have done in us, for us, and through us, in Jesus' name. Amen.

This Week's Prayer Guide

Sunday
"Christian humility does not consist in denying what there is of good in us; but in ... the consciousness that what we have of good is due to the grace of God" (Charles Hodge).

Monday
Fairness, kindness, loyalty, and humility are mentioned in Micah 6:8. In which of these virtues are you most likely to ask God for an increase? Talk with Him about it.

Tuesday
Pray with thanksgiving that God gives you opportunities every day, to demonstrate these virtues in your dealings with others.

Wednesday
Mildred Hill imagined that she was a nail on the wall and that upon her hung a picture of Jesus. People saw His face. They never saw the nail behind the picture. Meditate on these lines from her prayer song "God's Nail":

> Make me, O Lord, a nail upon the wall, fastened securely in its place;
> Then, from this thing, so common and so small, hang a bright picture of Thy face,
> That travelers may pause to gaze upon the loveliness depicted there …
> Let me be nothing but a nail upon the wall, holding Thy picture in its place.

Thursday
Think of an important accomplishment in your life. Practice telling the story to your grandchildren or to a group of young people. Be sure to give God credit for His involvement in your story.

Friday
How is God using you now that you may not be as strong and mobile as you used to be? Thank Him that you are still

useful. If you are still serving in the same way you always did, thank Him even more.

Saturday
Pray Mildred Hill's prayer again, or create your own similar prayer of humility.

CUPFUL #8

DOES GOD REALLY SPEAK?

> You will hear a voice behind you saying, "You should go this way."
> (Isaiah 30:21)

While sitting at my desk at work, the ringing in my ears gradually grew louder. I knew that I would not be able to sleep that night unless the noise stopped, so I called my doctor for an emergency appointment. He walked into the examination room and greeted me. "What is God telling you to do, that you're not doing?"

That was totally unexpected. First of all, I had gone there to get an opinion from a doctor not from a pastor, which he was not. We discussed his assumption, to determine if it was correct. After I failed to disprove my alarming disobedience, I changed my mind about a decision that had caused me some discomfort (stress). Since that day, more than twenty years ago, I have not experienced ringing in my ears.

God has a million ways to get our attention. The Dallas Ear Institute stated in a 2017 article that stress can trigger tinnitus (ringing in the ears). Then when the tinnitus itself causes more stress, a vicious cycle is created—ringing that causes anxiety that causes ringing! Who better than the doctor to explain this disturbing situation to me? I still wonder how he knew that my condition was more than physical.

God used a roundabout way to speak to me, and I might have missed His direction if I did not accept that there is purpose in everything He does. I imagine that He smiles when we are mindful enough to recognize the unusual ways in which He sends messages to direct our steps.

If you listen to Him closely through the written Word, and the Word spoken by His messengers, you will see and hear His directions clearly. Balaam refused to see, and he lived to regret it (see Num. 22:21–34). Even when those around you are confused, you will understand what God is saying to you, if you give Him your full attention.

PRAYER: Thank You, Lord, for the many different ways in which You communicate with us. Please help us to recognize Your directions clearly. In Jesus' name, Amen.

This Week's Prayer Guide

Sunday
"When every other voice is hushed, and in quietness we wait before Him, the silence of the soul makes more distinct the voice of God" (White, *The Ministry of Healing*, p. 58).

Monday
Prayer is a two-way conversation. You talk, God listens. God talks, you listen. Pray to learn the habit of listening patiently for His guidance.

Tuesday
"My sheep listen to my voice … and they follow me" (John 10:27). Pray for the willingness to obey what you already

know that He says in His Word. The more closely you follow, the more likely you are to hear His voice.

Wednesday
"He may speak in a dream, or in a vision at night, when people are in a deep sleep lying in their beds" (Job 33:15). God spoke to Joseph in dreams (Gen 37:8). He spoke to Daniel in visions (see Dan. 7). Pray to remain close enough to God so that you will always recognize His guidance in whatever form He sends it.

Thursday
It is easier to hear God when we're obedient, quiet, patient, and focused. Though sometimes He startles us, as He did Moses with the burning bush (see Exodus 3), or His disciples, who thought they saw a ghost on the lake (see Matt. 22:25–26). Pray that sudden or unusual situations will not distract you from recognizing God and hearing His voice.

Friday
Try to recognize God's voice today through likely sources (Christian broadcast, conversation with a friend, a song someone sings) and also through unlikely sources. Pray to be sensitive to His presence and His voice.

Saturday
In his sermon titled, "Speak, Lord," the nineteenth-century preacher Charles Haddon Spurgeon encourages us to reflect on other ways in which God speaks to us. Pray for the insight to hear Him.

> God often speaks to His children through His works. Are there not days when the mountains and the hills break forth before

us into singing and the trees of the field clap their hands because God is speaking by them?...

God also speaks to His children very loudly by His Providence ... Whether He caresses or chastises, there is a voice in all that He does. Oh, that we were not so deaf!...

But the Lord speaks to us chiefly through His Word ... There, in your still room, as you have been reading a chapter, have you not felt as if God spoke those words straight to your heart then and there?

CUPFUL #9

THE GOOD LIFE

> Respect the Lord and you will have a good life, one that is satisfying and free from trouble.
>
> (PROVERBS 19:23)

"He was extremely poor, yet he lived a rich life." Richard Glaubman wrote this statement about George Dawson, the old man who learned to read at age ninety-eight. Glaubman helped Dawson write his biography, which was titled, *Life Is So Good.*

Dawson, the grandson of a slave, was born in 1898 in Marshall, Texas. He began working on the farm at age four. At age twelve, he was hired to a neighboring farm to work for less than two dollars per week. He left home at age twenty-one, and spent his working life in hard labor, which ranged from picking cotton to crew work on the railroads. Riding the rails, he visited Mexico and Canada, and gained a glimpse of life outside his harsh world.

All the while, Dawson could read neither letters nor numbers. He never had the time to learn, although he had the desire. When he heard that adult-education classes were being taught a few blocks from his home, he attended. He learned the alphabet in two days, and wrote in cursive without first learning to print. His book was published when he was age 102; he died at age 103.

"Life is so good, and it gets better every day," he wrote. What was so good about Dawson's life? God enabled him to endure poverty, discrimination, and a host of other unwanted conditions. When the opportunity came, at the age of ninety-eight, his purpose and passion were still intact. He never lost the desire to live and to be productive. By the time he became an author, his troubles were behind him.

When God turns your troubles into triumphs, count your blessings, and enjoy the good life—the life of overcomers. Life is good when, by God's grace, you have endured the trials and can testify about the triumphs. Thank Him that you're still alive, and keep on expecting more of the good life, in His company.

PRAYER: Dear God, we thank for You for the good life You planned for us here, and in eternity. Help us not to give up, but to endure. In Jesus' name, Amen.

This Week's Prayer Guide

Sunday
"I want for people not to worry so much. Life ain't going to be perfect, but things will work out" (George Dawson).

Monday
Jesus said, "I came that they may have life and have it abundantly" (John 10:10). In what areas of life do you have abundance? Finances? Health? Friendships? Church family? Grandchildren? Thank God today, for whatever abundance there is in your life.

Tuesday
Some days are better than others, but God is good all the time. Pray to see God's goodness even when the day does not seem good.

Wednesday
You have had some good days: when God answered a prayer, when a loved one visited, when you received a pleasant surprise. You have not always said thanks. Lavish some praise on Him today for all those times when you should have, but you did not. Expect to have more of those good days.

Thursday
Meditate on these verses from "Yes, God Is Good," written by John Hampden Gurney:

> Yes, God is good, all nature says,
> By God's own hand with speech endued;
> And man, in louder notes of praise,
> Should sing for joy that God is good.
> For all Thy gifts we bless Thee, Lord,
> But chiefly for our heavenly food;
> Thy pard'ning grace, Thy quick'ning word,
> These prompt our song that God is good.

Friday
God's good life includes eternal life. Thank Him that you have access to the best life, through Jesus Christ, our Savior and Lord.

Saturday
Did you give up on a project because you thought you were too old? Let Dawson's story inspire you. Pray for the grace and strength to move forward in faith.

CUPFUL #10

UNFADING BEAUTY

> Your beauty should come from inside you—the beauty of a gentle and quiet spirit. That beauty will never disappear. It is worth very much to God.
>
> (1 PETER 3:4)

The Bible counsels that real beauty is revealed from the inside out. It displays itself in our attitude, in our deportment, and in our passion. This is the beauty that never disappears, and it is the beauty that God values. Lasting beauty!

> My beauty will last as long as I live; no dwindling of charm you will see.
> I have found a way to boost my appeal as the years take their toll on me.
> I'll point to the aging signs as they come, as trophies I've brought from the past:
> As lessons I've learned and lessons I've taught, for beauty with wisdom will last.
>
> I'll lean on my cane when my feet are tired, and walk far and fast as I can.
> Meeting new people and sharing their strength is part of my wise-beauty plan.

Older and Stronger

My aged lips will not get any thinner; they'll fly full like a ship's foremast
Cheering the young to live wisely and well, so their beauty and wisdom can last.

I'll tell my children and their children too, of the struggles which kept me strong;
I'll write for them, beautiful words of love which they can make into song;
For I know their beauty is influenced by the beauty they see in me;
Lord, help me display Your beauty and grace so they can copy me.

My beauty will last till the day I die, not because of human skill;
But because when my wisdom and glamor grow less, I trust God my lack to fill.
The challenge for all my dear friends and me when the vote of age is cast,
Is to balance good looks with godly wit, then beauty with wisdom will last.

—Dora Isaac Weithers

PRAYER: Heavenly Father, thank You for the gift of lasting, inner beauty. Please let it be seen in our character and caring attitude. Let the beauty of Jesus be seen in us, we pray in His worthy name. Amen.

This Week's Prayer Guide

Sunday
"Beautiful young people are accidents of nature but beautiful old people are works of art" (Eleanor Roosevelt).

Monday
Where does your inner beauty come from? What the apostle Paul refers to as the fruit of the Spirit turns out to be the very qualities people think of when they talk about inner beauty—love, joy, peace, patience, kindness, goodness, faithfulness, gentleness, and self-control. After we have accepted Jesus as Lord and are walking in the Holy Spirit, we will bear the fruit of the Spirit (see Gal. 5:22–23), which is perceived by others as inner beauty. Pray to cooperate with the Holy Spirit, who develops your beauty inside.

Tuesday
Do you ever stare at personal portraits that were taken in your younger days, and wonder where your beautiful features went? Thank God for your maturity and wisdom, which serve you better than the physical features that have diminished.

Wednesday
Smiling is a physical feature that reveals both inner and outer beauty. It also helps to change moods for the better. Pray for the grace to smile as often as possible, for your benefit and for the benefit of others.

Thursday
Sing or meditate on the words of this popular verse by Albert Orsborn:

> Let the beauty of Jesus be seen in me,
> All his wonderful passion and purity,
> O thou Spirit divine, all my nature refine,
> Till the beauty of Jesus be seen in me.

Friday

Nurture both your thriving inner beauty and your fading physical beauty. Pay attention to your hair, teeth, nails, skin—your total self. Thank God for the strength to take care of yourself, as well as you can. Pray for help in the areas where you need it.

Saturday

Thank God for at least two persons who modeled true (inner) beauty to you. If possible, let them know how they influenced your life.

CUPFUL #11

TESTIMONIES

> You are my source of strength, so I have been an example to others.
>
> (Psalm 71:7)

Have you ever noticed two or three people standing together, staring at you? I hope that doesn't worry you. They could be admiring you, wondering how you age so well. They may even be wondering if your faith in God is responsible for your graceful aging.

The psalmist lived a life of dependence on God. God had protected him in his childhood and youth, and was his refuge in old age. Still, he worried about the way his enemies would treat him. Eventually, based on his experience of God's care for him in the past, he trusted God to walk him through the rest of his life. He testified.

> "You are my source of strength, so I have been an example to many" (Ps. 71:7).
>
> "I will tell people how good you are. I will tell about all the times you saved me—too many times to count" (verse 15).
>
> "You have let me see troubles and hard times, but you will give me new life" (verse 20).
>
> "You will help me do even greater things. You will comfort me again!" (verse 21).

"My tongue will sing about your goodness all the time" (verse 24).

People are impressed when we maintain faith in God no matter what. They wonder about our church attendance, regular despite our aches and pains. They wonder how we remain focused and forgiving to those who offend us. Eventually, our stability helps them realize that God is our rock when our world seems to be shifting. He is our refuge when we need protection. He is our peace when we need to sleep at night.

Always testify about God's love. Tell how His promises lessened your worries. And to those who are watching, show your good side—the beauty of God's character within you, reflecting the satisfaction of His goodness all around you. He has been your strength throughout your life. He will not fail you now.

PRAYER: Eternal refuge, we thank You for the strength You have always provided. Please let our faith in You be a witness to all who wonder about the victories You have won, and will continue winning for us, in Jesus' name. Amen.

This Week's Prayer Guide

Sunday
"There are living upon our earth men who have passed the age of fourscore and ten. The natural results of old age are seen in their feebleness. But they believe God, and God loves them" (White, *Last Day Events*, p. 223).

Monday
The psalmist testifies, "You are my source of strength, so I have been an example to many (Ps. 71:17)." Who has been such an example to you? Thank God for that person's

influence on your life. Pray to be a similar influence on someone.

Tuesday
The Psalmist testifies, "You have let me see troubles and hard times, but you will give me new life" (71:20). What hard times have you had? Thank God that you survived. Add that story to your testimony.

Wednesday
The Psalmist also testifies, "My tongue will sing about your goodness" (verse 24). Sing one of your favorite hymns or try these popular lines written by William Ralph Featherstone, at age sixteen.

> "My Jesus, I love thee, I know thou art mine;
> For thee all the follies of sin I resign;
> My gracious Redeemer, my Savior art thou;
> If ever I loved thee, my Jesus, 'tis now."

Thursday
Ask God for courage to declare your testimony of God's goodness. Pray for the opportunity to tell someone soon.

Friday
What do you think most people will remember about you? Pray that starting today, the testimony of your life will be one worth remembering.

Saturday
How do you know that older people can be really happy? Reflect on the personal reasons you will give to someone who asks that question. Thank God today for whatever measure of joy there is in your life.

CUPFUL #12

EMBRACING CHANGE

> So Naomi ... came back from the hill country of Moab ... at the beginning of the barley harvest.
>
> (Ruth 1:22)

Naomi left Bethlehem for Moab in search of a better life. Unfortunately, she would have to retrace her steps. She left Bethlehem with family and potential, but after losing her husband and two sons, she returned, an older and less-able woman. Her hometown knew her by her name, which means *pleasantness,* but she came back feeling sad (Ruth 1:20–21). Still, it served her purpose to return home.

People like Naomi deserve commendation for embracing change even when it is uncomfortable, for not giving up when the odds are against them. Real success is fulfilling the God-given purpose for which He made us, and it is His hand that charts our course. When we are committed to fulfilling our purpose, we cannot be embarrassed to retrace our steps, if that is included in His plan. We must follow where God leads, even when we do not understand why.

When Naomi left Bethlehem, there was famine. Now that there was food, she was returning home to get her share. She returned with Ruth, her late son's widow. While she was losing family members in Moab, she was gaining favor with God. He used her for His purpose of positioning Ruth in the Messiah's lineage, and also to take care of her. Do you see why Naomi did not return as empty handed as she had thought? Do you see how changes that seem confusing can become enlightening when we see God in them?

Your change may or may not include a physical move. You may have to go back to an older, disciplinary lifestyle, to reconciliation in a former relationship, or to previous practices of prayer and Bible study, as you seek God's purpose. Accept His insight and be obedient to embrace the changes He arranges for you. His plans always work out in the interest of His children.

PRAYER: Heavenly Father, thank You for charting our course toward peace and fulfillment. Give us the courage to follow the changes You include for our benefit. In Jesus' name, Amen.

This Week's Prayer Guide

Sunday
"Nothing paralyzes our lives like the attitude that things can never change. We need to remind ourselves that God can change things" (Warren Wiersbe).

Monday
Is there any position or place or person that you are holding on to, because you think that stepping away would mean stepping backward? Whether or not it's so, pray for the courage to remain in God's will.

Tuesday
Naomi thought she was returning to Bethlehem empty-handed. Think of all that she still had. Pray for the

insight to realize that having faith in God means having a provider.

Wednesday
Ruth, the daughter-in-law who accompanied Naomi, knew that Naomi had no material possessions, but she told the older woman, "Your people will be my people. Your God will be my God" (Ruth 1:16). Has anyone been attracted to you because they want your God to be theirs? Pray that your relationship with God could influence others to want Him too.

Thursday
Could Naomi have been thinking about her losses when she returned home and said, "The Lord has made me sad?" (Ruth 1:21). Pray that your losses would become less and less important as you count your blessings.

Friday
Naomi has become a witness to people of all generations that no matter the changes we experience, God remains good. He can also use us as examples of His goodness. Sing or meditate on the first verse of a hymn written by Nahum Tate and Nicholas Brady:

> Through all the changing scenes of life, in trouble and in joy,
> the praises of my God shall still my heart and tongue employ.
> Of his deliv'rance I will boast, till all that are distressed,
> from my example comfort take and lay their griefs to rest.

Saturday
Pray, in your old age, for willingness to serve God with obedience and commitment wherever He places you.

CUPFUL #13

THE JOY OF OBEDIENCE

> Light and happiness shine on those
> who want to do right.
>
> (PSALM 97:11)

When Miss Holly retired, God impressed upon her that her purpose was to become an ardent student of the Bible, and to share the truth she found. She spent much of her extra time in singing, reading, and praying in private. Her aim was spiritual maturity—acknowledging and repenting of some un-Christ like habits she still had, and becoming a clean vessel for God to use.

In the midst of developing her faith, it seemed appropriate to invite a female friend to join her in Bible studies. But she was not as brave as she thought, and she procrastinated. Imagine her surprise when the friend initiated the conversation, and they began to study weekly. At first, Miss Holly was delighted at the prospect, but became disappointed when her friend refused to make a wholehearted commitment to Jesus. Still, Miss Holly's passion for sharing her faith did not diminish.

The two women continued praying and studying together. Miss Holly discovered that in her quest for information to share, her joy for Bible study increased, and she gained more spiritual light for her own journey. When we work for God at the tasks He assigns us, delays and disappointments cannot steal our joy. Obedience brings blessings. Blessings add to our happiness and satisfaction.

Do you ever express thanks for the personal benefits you receive from the effort you put into kingdom assignments for God and for others? You will soon realize that in addition to the long-term results you expect, there are many joyous rewards in the present. Strength of purpose, improved skills, confidence, and sweet fellowship are just few of the bonus blessings—blessings for you to enjoy!

PRAYER: Gracious God, we thank You for selecting us to serve. Please help us to enjoy the journey in obedience, as much as the reward. In Jesus' name, Amen.

This Week's Prayer Guide

Sunday
"When obedience to God contradicts what I think will give me pleasure, let me ask myself if I love Him" (Elisabeth Elliot).

Monday
The Bible describes itself as a healing tool (see Prov. 4:21). Which are you more likely to forget? Instructions from the doctor, or instructions from the Bible? Pray that you remember and be obedient to both.

Tuesday
Peter also compares the Word of God to milk, which nourishes our spirit (see 1 Peter 2:2). Pray that you never

outgrow your need of God's Word, to keep you growing spiritually.

Wednesday
The psalmist says that God's Word is a lamp (see Ps. 119:105), and our Scripture verse adds that light shines on those who do right. Pray to remain faithful to God's Word, so that His light will always shine on you.

Thursday
In addition to reading your Bible, ask your pastor or Bible teacher to help you obtain some study guides for more in-depth study. You can use them by yourself, or you may like to have a Bible-study partner. Pray today that God helps you find someone who is interested in studying with you.

Friday
Do you feel happy when you study the Bible? Do you miss it, if you go for a day without reading it? Pray that studying God's Word becomes your steady habit. Pray also for the faith to obey what you learn.

Saturday
This verse from Mary A. Lathbury's "Break Thou the Bread of Life" may open up your heart to hear from God. Sing or meditate on it, then read the Scripture verse for the last time, this week.

> Break Thou the Bread of Life, dear Lord, to me,
> As Thou didst break the loaves beside the sea;
> Beyond the sacred page I seek Thee, Lord;
> My spirit pants for Thee, O Living Word.

A SEVENTEENTH-CENTURY NUN'S PRAYER

(CREDITED TO MARGOT BENARY-ISBERT)

Lord, Thou knowest better than I know myself that I am growing older and will someday be old.

Keep me from the fatal habit of thinking that I must say something on every subject and on every occasion. Release me from the craving to straighten out everybody's affairs.

Make me thoughtful but not moody; helpful but not bossy. With my vast store of wisdom, it seems a pity not to use it all but thou knowest, Lord, that I want a few friends at the end.

Keep my mind free from the recital of endless details; give me wings to get to the point.

Seal my lips on my aches and pains. They are increasing and love of rehearsing them is becoming sweeter as the years go by. I dare not ask for grace enough to enjoy the tales of others' pains, but help me to endure them with patience.

I dare not ask for improved memory but for a growing humility and lessening cock sureness when my memory seems to clash with the memories of others. Teach me the glorious lesson that occasionally I may be mistaken.

Keep me reasonably sweet; I do not want to be a saint; some of them are so hard to live with. But a sour old person is one of the crowning works of the devil.

Give me the ability to see the good things in unexpected places and talents in unexpected people. And, give me, O Lord, the grace to tell them so. Amen.

Section Two
FAITH

"Let's do whatever will help each other
grow stronger in faith."

(Romans 14:19)

"Faith is a tremendously active principle
that always puts Jesus Christ first."

"Until we know Jesus, God is merely a concept,
and we can't have faith in Him. But once we hear
Jesus say, "He who has seen Me has seen the Father"
(John 14:9) we immediately have something that is
real, and our faith is limitless."

"Faith is the entire person in the right relationship
with God through the power of the Spirit of Jesus
Christ."

(Oswald Chambers, 1927)

CUPFUL #14

STRONGER FAITH

> But we are not those who turn back and are lost. No, we are the people who have faith and are saved.
>
> (HEBREWS 10:39)

There are three virtues that last forever (1 Cor. 13:13), and the first one mentioned is faith — "abiding trust in God and His promises" (AMP). In our early years, faith was introduced to us as the expectation that God will answer our prayers. We asked, we believed, we expected, and when the answer came, we had proven our faith.

Later, there were times when we asked, believed and expected, but there were obstacles between us and the answer. Instead of clearing the path, like we knew He could, God seemed bent on teaching us lessons in patience, in selflessness, in surrender. In the midst of our struggle to hold on while we wait, He answered in response to our shaken, but stronger, faith.

In our more mature years, we accept that asking, believing and expecting do not always guarantee the outcome we requested. Experience has taught us that stronger faith continues to trust God, no matter how different the answer is from our expectations. We learn from the heroes of faith in Hebrews 11, that when the promise does not seem to materialize, it is because "God planned something better for us. He wanted to make us perfect" (verse 40).

The more we exercise it, the more our faith continues to grow. "We are not those who turn back and are lost." We have testimonies to share, of how our faith has been rewarded in the past. We are those who "encourage each other and help each other grow stronger in faith" (1 Thess. 5:11).

> **In our more mature years, we accept that asking, believing and expecting do not always guarantee the outcome we requested. Experience has taught us that stronger faith continues to trust God, no matter how different the answer is from our expectations.**

PRAYER: Loving God, faith in You has given meaning to our lives. We pray that our faith grows stronger and stronger every day. In Jesus' name, Amen.

This Week's Prayer Guide

Sunday
"Faith never knows where it is being led, but it loves and knows the One who is leading" (Oswald Chambers).

Monday
Have you ever turned back on God in your walk with Him? Maybe you did, even while you attended church regularly. Confess your weaknesses, accept God's forgiveness, and pray that your faith in God will increase daily.

Tuesday
Ephesians 2: 8 explains that faith is useful because it reaches for, and holds onto, God's grace, which saves us: "You have been saved by grace because you believed. You did not save yourselves; it was a gift from God." Thank God for the gift of salvation through His grace.

Wednesday
Faith believes in God's promises even when trials become burdensome. "You know that when your faith is tested, you learn to be patient in suffering. If you let that patience work in you … you will be mature and complete" (James 1:3, 4). Pray for strong faith to persevere.

Thursday
Sing or meditate on these verses written by an unknown author.

> I have decided to follow Jesus. (Three times)
> No turning back, no turning back.
> Though none go with me, I still will follow. (Three times)
> No turning back, no turning back.

Friday
Hebrews 11:6 states that "Without faith, it is impossible to please God." Pray for God's Holy Spirit within you to sustain your faith.

Saturday
Repeat Thursday's activity. Pray for a faith strong enough to influence others.

CUPFUL #15

CONTENTMENT

> Right now I am calm and quiet, like a child after nursing, content in its mother's arms.
>
> (PSALM 131:2)

Knowing and befriending a centenarian was one of the rare privileges God granted me. Mother Louise was the model of healthy aging in our community. Even more than her physical abilities, her mental state was impressive.

At age 101, she recited songs and Bible verses in her conversation, and recited lines from Thomas Gray's *Elegy Written in a Country Churchyard*. She was not an old soul needing encouragement. She wore courage and inspiration on her sleeve. She maintained a refreshing laughter, which suggested that life was still good all the way up to her final, 103rd year.

When asked about the reasons for her health, longevity, and obvious joy, Mother Louise pointed upward. God was her first answer. She credited Him for the strength that enabled her to live and serve, including raising and educating twelve children. "There is no reason to be unhappy," she said. "There may not be much of material possessions, but a spirit of contentment will help you find many, many reasons to be happy."

Contentment

How do you obtain that spirit of contentment during the difficulties that come with aging? The psalmist likened himself to an infant who had been frustrated, and perhaps in discomfort, who fed from mother's breast and became calm and contented. Give your worries, regrets, disappointments, and fears to God, then lay your head on His breast, and feed on His promises. Experience the sweetness of contentment.

PRAYER: Dear God, give us an appetite for Your promises, so that we might eat and drink 'til our minds and spirits are contented. We thank You, in Jesus' name. Amen.

This Week's Prayer Guide

Sunday
"I have held many things in my hands, and have lost them all; but whatever I have placed in God's hands, that I still possess" (Martin Luther).

Monday
Psalm 131 has only three verses. The first is an expression of humility: "Lord, I don't feel proud. I don't see myself as better than others. I am not thinking about doing great things or reaching impossible goals." What are your thoughts? Pray to know and focus on the goals that God has in mind for you.

Tuesday
Our Scripture verse is the second in the Psalm. It pictures a position of contentment: "No, right now I am calm and quiet, like a child after nursing, content in its mother's arms." Close your eyes and imagine yourself in such a contented state. Pray for God to favor you with such a restful, satisfied feeling.

Wednesday
Are there any anxieties, fears, or doubts that sometimes rob you of a contented spirit? Ask God to take them away and give you His peace.

Thursday
The last verse in Psalm 131 expresses trust, which helps the spirit of contentment: "Israel, trust in the Lord. Trust in him now and forever!" Just like the baby who feeds from his mother's breast and feels satisfied, so the believer feeds on God's Word and feels contented. Pray to experience a sense of joy when you read and claim God's promises.

Friday
Think on these words from "Contentment," the author identified only as V.C.:

> I am happy, O so happy at God's side,
> I am walking in His presence, satisfied.
> Hallelujah, hallelujah,
> I am walking in His presence, satisfied.

Saturday
Pray to be contented for as long as you live. Pray for God to teach you how to share your spirit of contentment.

CUPFUL #16

FAITHFULNESS IN OLDER MEN

> Teach the older men to have self-control, to be serious, and to be wise. They must be strong in faith, in love, and in patience.
>
> (TITUS 2:2)

Paul specifically admonished Christian older men to grow in these three graces—faith, love, and patience.

John Calvin, the sixteenth century reformer wrote, "It is with 'faith' that we worship God—no prayer, no work of piety, can be severed from 'faith.'" He added that faith displays itself in love to our neighbors, and that faith cannot endure without patience. All three virtues combine in the character of the older man.

The older Christian man is charming in a different way from when he was young. His self-importance fades, and Christlikeness becomes his main appeal. Women and children are attracted to his discretion and restraint. He laughs with them and engages them in lively conversation without any hint of vulgarity.

His deportment, whether classy or casual, summons respect, and he respects the value of others. Influenced by

God's Holy Spirit, he controls his appetites as well as his anger and disgust at the frustrations of life.

The three abiding virtues of "faith, hope, and love" (1 Cor. 13:13) are embedded in the godly older man. Faith and love remain vibrant; and hope is undergirded with patience. His most cherished hope is heaven and the physical presence of God. He remains faithful through suffering, while modeling His Savior's love and grace. God honors the godly old man and young people esteem him.

PRAYER: Thank You, God, for faithful older men, whose virtues inspire faithfulness in the younger generation. May their lives demonstrate Your love and strength in a way that honors You. In Jesus' name, Amen.

This Week's Prayer Guide

Sunday
"Faithful servants never retire. You can retire from your career, but you will never retire from serving God" (Rick Warren).

Monday
Which of the three virtues—faith, hope, patience—do you think the older person needs most? Pray to grow in each one every day.

Tuesday
Do you think that older people should be respected just because of their age, or depending on the kind of life they have been living? Pray and live in such a way that folks around you will have reason to like and respect you.

Wednesday
Think of an older man in the Bible or from the community, dead or alive, whose life influenced yours. Which of his virtues do (did) you admire most? Pray to live a life that leaves a positive influence on others.

Thursday
Do you believe that, generally speaking, men struggle more than women to live holy lives? Paul lets us know that God has grace enough save all of us, even those who have harder struggles. He states in 1 Corinthians 15:10, "I worked harder than all the other apostles. (But I was not really the one working. It was God's grace that was with me.)" Give thanks that there is grace enough for every struggle.

Friday
Sing one stanza from "Faith of Our Fathers" by Frederick W. Faber:

> Faith of our fathers we will love
> Both friend and foe in all our strife,
> And preach thee, too, as love knows how,
> By kindly words and virtuous life.
> Faith of our fathers, holy faith!
> We will be true to thee till death!

Saturday
Read the devotional again. Thank God for giving us the standard by which to measure and improve our lives.

CUPFUL #17

GOODNESS IN OLDER WOMEN

> Guide older women into lives of reverence so they end up as neither gossips nor drunks, but models of goodness.
>
> (Titus 2:3, MSG)

The Christian old woman is attractive, not necessarily because of the graceful fashion she wears, but rather because her entire being is endowed with the inner, timeless *"beauty of a gentle and quiet spirit, which is very precious in the sight of God"* (1 Peter 3:4, KJV).

    Her disposition is sacred, not sanctimonious, because she credits her grooming to the influence of God's Holy Spirit within her. She displays godliness in her fashion style, in her speech, in her interaction with others, and in her general conduct. Children and youth admire her efforts to remain relatable, as she laughs and learns with them. By her honest counsel, based on her experiences, she guides younger adult women through the mundane struggle for survival to the permeating joy of virtuous, productive womanhood. She is an enlightening ray of sunshine.

Compliments, not criticisms, become her watchword, since she has learned the value of building up instead of breaking down. Gratitude, not grumbling, becomes her main expression, because she counts more blessings than burdens and blunders.

Her happiness comes from divine strength that maintains her beauty within, not from external products. She renounces intoxicating liquors and harmful drugs. She feeds her body with healthy nutrients; her mind and spirit, with godly teachings.

The Christian older woman is the beacon of hope to those who fear aging. She is her Savior's exhibit of His ageless love, goodness, joy, peace, and comfort.

PRAYER: Thank You, God, that in Your great and wonderful world, You reserved a place for women. May their lives represent Your goodness, gentleness, and grace in a way that brings You honor and glory. In Jesus' name, Amen.

This Week's Prayer Guide

Sunday
"The Christian does not think God will love us because we are good, but that God will make us good because He loves us" (C.S. Lewis).

Monday
"Lives of reverence!" There seems to be a high and holy calling on the lives of Christian women. Women, pray for God's strength and wisdom to live the holy life God expects of you.

Tuesday
Paul wanted the women to model holiness in speech and conduct, and to avoid drinking wine in excess. Pray that

today, despite the distinguished public positions some godly women hold, they will continue to focus on being Christian in their behavior.

Wednesday
Think of an older woman in the Bible or in the community, dead or alive, whose life influenced yours. Which of her virtues do (did) you admire most? Pray to live a life that leaves a positive influence on others.

Thursday
It is easy for older people striving to be holy, to appear self-righteous. They forget how to deal with sinners in their homes and communities. Pray for God to remind us how He forgave our youthful mistakes. Ask Him for tolerance to love and help the immature Christian.

Friday
Ponder these thoughts, written by Ellen White, about women committed to Christ: "All ... should have the Martha and the Mary attributes blended—a willingness to minister and a sincere love of the truth. Self and selfishness must be put out of sight. God calls for earnest women workers who are prudent, warmhearted, tender, and true to principle" (*Testimony Treasures*, vol. 2, p. 405).

Saturday
Thank God that men and women can help each other uphold the God-given standards by which we should live.

CUPFUL #18

GOD CAN DO ANYTHING

> [Elizabeth] is very old, but she is going to have a son ... Everyone thought she could not have a baby but ... God can do anything!
>
> (LUKE 1: 36–37)

There were five instances of healed barrenness recorded before Elizabeth's. The women of favor were Sarah, Rebekah, Rachel, Manoah's wife, and Hannah, in the Old Testament. In the number six spot was Elizabeth, whose prayer was answered with the conception of John the Baptist. He became the announcer to the world that Jesus, the seventh miraculous birth, was the Messiah.

Elizabeth and her husband devoted their lives to God. Her barrenness seemed to exclude them from God's favor and even exposed Elizabeth to disgrace; but in God's time, although they had passed child-bearing years, He delivered their blessing. With Him, all things are possible.

Our legacy, like Elizabeth's, could be a legacy of trust—trusting in God to do what's best no matter how long He delays the answer to our prayers. The real miracle is in having our blessing delivered at exactly the right time.

Is there a solution to a lifelong problem we are still experiencing? What if He wants our children to witness, rather than just hear from us, how He performed the impossible on our behalf? He may want them to learn from us how to maintain trust in Him, even when their blessing seems delayed. Whatever His reason, we can trust an all-wise God to act according to His schedule.

God is never too late with the fulfillment of a promise; for with Him, all things are possible. Blessings in your old age are evidence to your witnesses that God does not forget His aging saints, and that faithfulness and trust bring rewards.

PRAYER: Heavenly Father, You have a proven record of delivering blessings at the time they are most needed. May we erase our doubts and fears by turning to Your Word for reminders of Your goodness. In Jesus' name, Amen.

This Week's Prayer Guide

Sunday
"I used to ask God to help me. Then I asked if I might help Him. I ended up by asking God to do His work through me" (Hudson Taylor).

Monday
Every young Jewish bride, including Elizabeth, prayed for a male child. God answered Elizabeth when she was an old woman. Pray for the patience to wait on God, even when He does not answer immediately.

Tuesday
God can do anything. Ask Him today to do something you have not asked for before—something that will bring honor to Him, something you will be happy to mention in a future testimony. Pray a prayer of faith.

Wednesday
Ephesians 3:20: "With God's power working in us, he can do much, much more than anything we can ask or think of." Think of times when you watched God do more than you expected. Thank Him.

Thursday
Do you trust God enough to believe that even when He does not give what you ask for, He will supply what you need? Thank Him that He gives according to His riches (see Phil. 4:19).

Friday
"Everyone thought that she could not ... but ... God can do anything" (Luke 1:37). Persevere in prayer, no matter what others think.

Saturday
While we are waiting on God, it is important that, like Elizabeth, we maintain our faith and trust in Him. Meditate on the first stanza of "'Tis So Sweet to Trust in Jesus," by Louisa M. R. Stead:

> Tis so sweet to trust in Jesus,
> Just to take him at his word;
> Just to rest upon his promise,
> Just to know, "Thus saith the Lord."
>
> Refrain:
> Jesus, Jesus, how I trust him!
> How I've proved him o'er and o'er!
> Jesus, Jesus, precious Jesus!
> O for grace to trust him more!

CUPFUL #19

A PRAYER FOR JOY

> Your help made me so happy. Give me that joy again.
> Make my spirit strong and ready to obey you.
>
> (PSALM 51:12)

The pastor's wife had lost her joy until she attended a seminar on spiritual gifts. (Spiritual gifts are special abilities that God's Holy Spirit gives to each believer). She was worried that she had fallen out of love with Jesus, because it seemed that something in her life had gone missing.

Her primary spiritual gift was hospitality, and she exercised that gift, mainly by inviting folks to her home for Sabbath lunch. Recently, her husband had been moved from the position of church pastor to become a denominational executive. Because she travelled with her husband on weekends, Sabbath lunches were not always possible, and she missed having that opportunity to serve.

Then she learned in her class on spiritual gifts that it is God's Spirit who gives the special abilities, and it is He who places believers where He wants them to serve. In her case, she had been moved out of her comfort zone because God was offering her another opportunity for service, in another capacity. She soon began to facilitate afternoon sessions on hospitality, in the same churches where her husband delivered the morning message, and her joy returned.

The psalmist makes it clear that joy comes from God. The story of the pastor's wife affirms that one of the ways we experience joy is by accepting opportunities to do whatever God gives us the ability to do. Sometimes we do not willfully disobey God; we just neglect to pay attention to the duty He gives us, and then we wonder why we are not happy.

What special ability has God given you? Do not think only in terms of what you have always done. What new opportunities is He placing in your path? Let Him boost your joy by bringing out the special abilities within you, which you have not even noticed.

Do not limit yourself with regard to the ways in which God could use you. He has put gifts within you, for different times, even in different seasons of life. The same Holy Spirit who gives gifts also gives joy (see Gal. 5: 22). Be obedient to the task(s) that God has assigned you, and be ready to say what makes you so happy, because folks will ask.

PRAYER: God, the source of our joy, please make and keep us happy, by showing and enabling us to do whatever You want us to do. In Jesus' name, Amen.

This Week's Prayer Guide

Sunday
"If you have no joy, there's a leak in your Christianity somewhere" (Billy Sunday).

Monday
When David committed the sin of adultery with Bathsheba, he had regrets. He prayed, "Let me hear sounds of joy and happiness again" (verse 8). Confess any sin you might be cherishing, so that it will not prevent you from experiencing all of God's joy.

Tuesday
Think. When you are unhappy, is it because God takes away your joy, or because you have not accepted His joy? Pray to maintain fellowship with Him. As long as you are in fellowship with Him, you have access to His joy.

Wednesday
We tell children that they make God happy when they obey Him. The truth is, God makes us happy when we obey Him. Pray for the awareness to hear, understand, and obey what He wants you to do.

Thursday
Pray that God will use you and your skills for His glory, that He will keep you occupied so that you are not idle. Pray that you allow Him to maintain His joy within you.

Friday
Sing or meditate on Joseph Carlson's song "If You Want Joy":

> If you want joy, real joy, wonderful joy,
> Let Jesus come into your heart;
> If you want joy, real joy, wonderful joy,
> Let Jesus come into your heart;
> Your sins He'll wash away, your night He'll turn to day,
> Your life He'll make over anew;
> If you want joy, real joy, wonderful joy,
> Let Jesus come into your heart.

Saturday
Pray that you always look to God as your source of joy, and that you always receive the joy He gives.

CUPFUL #20

LOVING AND FORGIVING

"But I will make you pure, and you will never be ashamed again!" This is what the Lord God said.

(EZEKIEL 16:63)

God was betrayed by the people He chose to represent Him. To the prophet Ezekiel He described them as an unfaithful woman. He found her in a field, abandoned by her mother, He said. He nurtured her through healthy childhood and adulthood. He married her, provided her with food, fine clothes, and jewelry. He made her popular. Then she cheated on Him.

Repeatedly, God's people had worshipped false gods and surrendered to the influence of pagan nations. Sometimes, they behaved worse than their heathen friends, and their sins resulted in sufferings. Yet God remained their God.

What about us? Are we unfaithful to God? Have we ignored His love and given our affection to a world that does not love us? Have we given Him a bad name by fretting and complaining despite His provision for us?

Let's confess and repent from our sins, and have faith that He will forgive us (see 1 John 1:9). He will free us from the guilt of infidelity and restore us to a relationship of mutual love between Him and us. Our God remains faithful despite our unfaithfulness!

Now it is your turn to forgive the person who betrayed you or wronged you in any other way. Nobody's offense toward you can hurt you to the degree that your offenses against God have hurt Him. Forgiveness will never cost you as much as it cost God to forgive you. Love Him with all your might by loving and forgiving others.

PRAYER: Dear God, we thank You for Your goodness in loving first, unconditionally, and always. Thanks also for the opportunity to experience and extend the freedom that comes with forgiveness. In Jesus' name, Amen

This Week's Prayer Guide

Sunday
"The joy of pardon has a voice louder than the voice of sin. God's voice speaking peace is the sweetest music an ear can hear" (Charles Haddon Spurgeon).

Monday
God knows everything about us, and loves us anyway. Pray that like Him, even though we hate the sin, we learn to love the sinner.

Tuesday
God describes His relationship with His people as a love relationship. Pray that you will never be unfaithful to Him.

Wednesday
God's forgiveness cost Him the death of His Son Jesus on the cross. Has it cost you as much as it cost God to forgive

any of your offenders? Thank Him, again and again, for His forgiveness toward you.

Thursday
What do you owe to Jesus for saving you? Pray that you accept Him with your whole heart as your Savior from sin, and as Lord of your life.

Friday
Thank God for the sentiments expressed in this hymn by James McGranahan. The song title and first line are the same.

> God has forgiven all my sins;
> Behind His back they all are cast.
> He'll never call to mind again
> The sins He vanquished in the past.
> My sins were like a heavy stone
> God cast and buried in the sea.
> As east so far from west is thrown,
> My sins have been removed from me!

Saturday
Is there someone you need to forgive? Pray to share with that person the love and the forgiveness that you have received from God.

CUPFUL #21

DON'T BE AFRAID

> Don't worry—I am with you. Don't be afraid—I am your God. I will make you strong and help you.
>
> (Isaiah 41:10)

It took some time for me to understand why week after week, my mother was refusing to go to church. Having prepared her clothes the day before, and seeming to be in bright spirits and good health, she would surprise me when it was time to get dressed. She would simply inform me, "I'm not going today."

After a few weeks, I discovered the reason. She would forget why her clothes were hanging in plain sight, and she would put them away. Alzheimer's had robbed her of the ability to be as organized as she had been before, so she would store different parts of her outfit in different places, and not remember. Forgetting frustrated her. In order to avoid the worry and regain her peace, she stopped trying to remember and settled for not going to church.

There are many reasons to be frightened in our old age, but God counsels us not to be afraid or discouraged. He is with us in our confusion, and He promises to help. He is mighty in strength of understanding (see Job 36:5). He is

Don't Be Afraid

wise. He knows when we mean well although we mess up, and He still loves and cares.

What you think about Him *now* determines whether you trust Him to care for you *then*. Do you think He is great enough and caring enough to maintain you if your mind becomes feeble? Do you believe His promise that He will never leave you nor forsake you? Focus on Him now and trust in His promises. "Don't worry," He says. "Don't be afraid." He's wise enough to improvise for the help you need both now and then. Who else do you know, with certainty, will always be there for you?

> **There are many reasons to be frightened in our old age, but God counsels us not to be afraid or discouraged. He is with us in our confusion, and He promises to help.**

PRAYER: Heavenly Father, we love You because You are strong when we are weak. Please help us to trust in Your love and Your grace always. In Jesus' name, Amen.

This Week's Prayer Guide

Sunday
"Only he who can say, 'The Lord is the strength of my life' can say, 'Of whom shall I be afraid?'" (Alexander MacLaren).

Monday
You don't have to be afraid of Alzheimer's or any other sickness. God will be with you no matter what. Pray for a sound mind, and for God to provide the help you need. While you can, follow your doctor's instructions for good mental health.

Tuesday

Alzheimer's is not the only thing that scares older people; anxiety and panic attacks are also common among the aging. Pray for the presence of mind to run to Him when you recognize the worry. God can provide comfort through your recalling of hymns and promises you learned throughout the years.

Wednesday

Did you know that along with prayer, there are physical ways to lessen worry immediately? Perhaps a short walk, some deep breaths of fresh air, a good laugh with someone. Look for opportunities to relax and enjoy life. Ask for human help and trust God to sustain you.

Thursday

God will always love you. He promises to be with you always and never leave you (see Deut. 31:8). Meditate on that promise now: "Do not be afraid or discouraged, for the Lord will personally go ahead of you. He will be with you; he will neither fail you nor abandon you."

Friday

Sing or meditate on the words of "Why Worry" by Alfred B. Smith:

> Why worry, when you can pray?
> Trust in Jesus, He knows the way.
> Don't be a doubting Thomas, just lean upon His promise.
> Why worry, worry, worry, worry when you can pray.

Saturday

Meditate on another song or Bible promise that God used to comfort you in the past. If you cannot think of one, use our memory text for this week. Pray that He establishes it in your memory.

CUPFUL #22
WORSHIP RESPONSES

> With praise and thanksgiving they sang to the Lord:
> "He is good; his love toward Israel endures forever."
>
> (EZRA 3:11)

The children of Israel had completed the foundation for the new temple, and the mood of celebration filled the air in a variety of sounds. The younger people shouted for joy. Some who had returned from Babylonian captivity had not been privileged to worship in the first temple. Seeing the foundation of the new structure was enough to make them rejoice. They looked forward to experiencing temple worship the way their parents did.

But in the crowd were some of the older people who remembered the past: the first temple, which was more exquisite than the one they were building, and the disobedience and idolatry that preceded their capture. They cried tears of regret over past misdeeds as well as tears of gratitude to God for their survival.

In the same worship celebration there were different responses, based on different experiences. But all were singing of God's goodness. Is it possible for the young and old to worship God differently, but with the same intensity?

While we might insist on the sacredness and reverence, we knew "back in the day," let us appreciate that heartfelt responses from different hearts will not always look and sound the same. Some may bow silently, overwhelmed by the goodness of God, while others shout a loud amen, with raised hands begging for more of His presence.

> Is it possible for the young and old to worship God differently, but with the same intensity?

God listens to your heart. Focus completely on Him so that other people's response to Him will not distract from your absolute praise. He accepts the mingled sentiments of worshippers as sweet incense, and He identifies the perfume of adoration that is distinctly yours.

> Let us appreciate that heartfelt responses from different hearts will not always look and sound the same.

PRAYER: Holy Father, thank you for Your Holy Spirit who presents our praises and prayers in worship, in a manner that pleases You. In Jesus' name, Amen.

This Week's Prayer Guide

Sunday
"Those who invest more in a relationship with Jesus will have a greater sense of rejoicing in Him" (Crystal McDowell).

Monday
Do you express praise in public worship with shouts of hallelujah, amen, praise the Lord? Or do you participate

just by listening? Pray to focus on God and respond appropriately, every time.

Tuesday
Does it disturb you that some people shout or stand when you think they should not? Pray that nothing distracts you when you worship God.

Wednesday
Have you noticed that some young people take their worship seriously? They show it both by their performance and by their attentiveness in their seats. Pray for them. Call them by name.

Thursday
Habakkuk 2:20 says, "But the Lord is in his holy temple, so the whole earth should be silent in his presence." That means we are listening. Psalm 100:1 says, "Make a joyful noise unto the Lord (KJV)." That's when it is time to express our praise. Pray to get the greatest worship benefit possible, from both the silence and the noise.

Friday
Meditate on the beloved psalm of praise, Psalm 150:

> **Praise the LORD!** Praise God in his Temple!
> Praise him in heaven, his strong fortress!
> Praise him for the great things he does! Praise him for all his greatness!
> Praise him with trumpets and horns! Praise him with harps and lyres!
> Praise him with tambourines and dancing!
> Praise him with stringed instruments and flutes!

Praise him with loud cymbals! Praise him with crashing cymbals!

Everything that breathes, praise the LORD! Praise the LORD!

Saturday

Pray for the courage to use different expressions of praise in your personal devotional time. Pray for a blessed, joyful worship experience every day.

CUPFUL #23

GOD'S INTERVENTION

> You planned to do something bad to me. But really …
> God's plan was to use me to save the lives
> of many people.
>
> (GENESIS 50:20)

Instead of a plastic or light-metal shower curtain rod, the builder decided to use a heavy steel tube. He convinced me that because it would not bend or break, it would never need to be replaced. Fast forward a few years. During a repainting of the bathroom, the steel tube fell and shattered the lid of the toilet tank. My bathroom turned ugly and inconvenient.

The next morning I awoke to the thought that had I ever slipped coming out of the shower, I would have grabbed the shower curtain for support. I imagined the steel pipe landing on my forehead, knocking me backward and crashing my head onto the solid ceramic tiles. It was clear to me that God sometimes allows bad things to happen in order to prevent something worse.

It was cruel for Joseph to be thrown into a well, but that was the way God chose to save him from an early death (Gen. 37:18–22). It was unfair for him to be imprisoned innocently, but outside of prison, he might never have met the butler who introduced him to the pharaoh who set him up to feed his family in the midst of a famine (see Gen. 41). Despite the jealousy, hostility, slavery, and false accusations he suffered, he lived to tell his brothers who were the cause of his troubles, "You intended to harm me, but God intended it all for good."

Stop blaming and resenting and fretting about bad things that happened to you in the past. Change your perspective. Express gratitude for a God who intervened by allowing you to lose some things that might have destroyed you. According to His purpose, He spared you from worse. Having survived despite all your setbacks, you have proof that He knows what is best for you.

PRAYER: Heavenly Father, thank You for Your intervention in our everyday situations. We surrender completely to You, so that even when the good seems bad, Your purpose for our lives will prevail. In Jesus' name, Amen.

This Week's Prayer Guide

Sunday
"The sooner we stop taking the little things for granted, the more we'll realize how involved God is in our lives" (Sonya Downing).

Monday
Is there anyone you have blamed (or are blaming) for a negative incident in your life? Ask God for His grace to forgive, and for His grace to smile when you see or remember that person.

Tuesday
Do you have a list of people who helped you achieve good outcomes in your life? We often complain more than we

God's Intervention

give thanks. Thank God again for putting some good people in your life.

Wednesday
It was Joseph's own brothers who meant to do him harm, but when he found himself in a position to help them, he forgot all the evil they did, and he was kind to them. Pray that no matter what you suffer on account of other people's actions, you will focus on God's goodness. Thank Him for helping you to endure and survive.

> **Pray that no matter what you suffer on account of other people's actions, you will focus on God's goodness.**

Thursday
Thank God for forgiving you when you have caused pain to other people in the past. Focus on His love and compassion.

Friday
Thank God for His promise in Romans 8:28. If it has not already come true in your life, watch for it to happen. "We know that in everything God works for the good of those who love him. These are the people God chose, because that was his plan."

Saturday
Nothing that happened to Joseph altered God's plan for his life. God told him in his teens that he would become a leader (see Gen. 37:5–9). And he did, despite his pit and prison experiences (see Gen. 41:41). Thank God that He will also complete what He began in you.

CUPFUL #24

HOLD ME

> I stay close to you, and you hold me with your powerful arm.
>
> (Psalm 63:8)

Sometimes the road gets very dark, I can't see up ahead;
I wonder should I grope along or turn around instead.
I pray that You would shine a light, make the pathway clear,
Or clearly speak one promise that would take away my fear.
But if I do not hear You; if I do not see a light,
I'm still safe when You reach out and hold me through the night.

Sometimes my heart is aching from the wounds caused by my foes;
I rest and wait for time to heal me, as the saying goes.
I recall how much You suffered though You had hurt no one.
I pray for courage to forgive, the same as You have done.
Then I feel Your comfort flowing, pouring down like rain,
As You reach out and hold me, and heal me from my pain.

And then sometimes I'm tired of the struggles of the day:
The rising cost of living, and bills more than I can pay,
The ladders that I try to climb, the many slips and falls,

The hustling and the bustling, and the schedules and close calls.
I fear that I would lose my mind, have no more strength to give,
'Till You reach out and hold me, and renew my will to live.

You have held me, loving Jesus, safely all through the years;
Held me when I was cheerful, held me when I shed sad tears.
I know that I'm still standing only 'cause You hold me now;
And even as You hold me, in sweet gratitude I bow.
I cuddle in Your goodness; nothing can pull me away;
I'm safe because you hold me. In Your love I want to stay.

(Dora Isaac Weithers)

PRAYER: Thank You, God, for not letting me go. In Jesus' name, Amen.

This Week's Prayer Guide

Sunday
"Lord, I'm going to hold steady on to You and You've got to see me through" (Harriet Tubman).

Monday
Christian Ministry Leader, Joni Eareckson Tada, has been paralyzed from the shoulder down. She says, "God has chosen not to heal me, but to hold me." Pray for such wisdom to choose God's embrace over any other situation that may be unpleasant.

Tuesday
Thank God for holding and sustaining you through all kinds of situations, including those mentioned in the poem: spiritual darkness, heartache, everyday struggles, sadness, and even joy.

Wednesday
Pray for faith to believe that God is holding you, and to live like you believe it.

Thursday
Are you maintaining closeness with God? Do you ever feel Him holding you? Pray to experience and maintain a close friendship with Him.

Friday
Think on these lines from "Jesus Is a Friend of Mine" by John Henry Sammis:

> Why should I charge my soul with care? The wealth of ev'ry mine
> Belongs to Christ, God's Son and Heir, And He's a Friend of mine.
> Chorus:
> "Yes, He's a Friend of mine, and He with me doth all things share;
> Since all is Christ's, and Christ is mine, why should I have a care?
> For Jesus is a Friend of mine.

Saturday
Pray to appreciate and enjoy all the blessings that come with intimate fellowship between you and God. Think and talk about it, continually.

CUPFUL #25

THE LIVING SERMON

> Dorcas ... was always doing good things for people.
> (Acts 9:36)

When Leta was a little girl, the story of Tabitha (also called Dorcas) was her favorite. Looking at the story through her adult eyes, it became clear that Dorcas's daily life— "always doing good things for people and giving money to those in need" (Acts 9:36) was a living sermon. Following in the footsteps of the Bible woman, Leta decided that her purpose was also to a live a sermon every day.

Leta could not sew coats like Dorcas did, but she developed a passion for helping people in any way she could. In her retirement years, she chose to serve her community as a counselor and motivator to young adults who needed guidance and practical help to advance in their careers. Making a difference in the lives of others gave her joy and the impetus to do as much as she could.

When Dorcas got sick and died, the people created a display of the clothes she had sewed for them. It must have been quite impressive. But Leta is still alive and is gladly witnessing a partial display of the work she has done in the lives of those whom she has helped. Many have returned to express thanks and even to present gifts. As much as she appreciates the earthly gestures, her greater privilege is to perform her service in honor and gratitude to God.

What are you doing in your later years, with the talent and skills that God has gifted to you? For what do people admire you? You have the chance to sermonize Jesus in your attitudes, your words, and your deeds. You are a living example of His compassion and graciousness. Through your love and kindness to others, they will see Christ in you. You are not just taking up space. You are keeping the faith and preaching it to others by your Christian lifestyle.

PRAYER: Dear Lord, we thank You for the privilege of preaching Your goodness by the way we live our lives. May it become a habit. In Jesus' name, Amen.

This Week's Prayer Guide

Sunday
"I'd rather see a sermon than hear one any day" (From the poem "Sermons We See" by Edgar A. Guest).

Monday
The sentiment in these lines from the hymn "Father, Lead Me Day by Day" by John Page Hopps make a good morning prayer as we prepare to live our sermon:

Father, lead me day by day, ever in Thine own good way;
Teach me to be pure and true, show me what I ought to do.

Tuesday
Besides sewing coats like Dorcas did, what are some everyday actions that could serve as sermons? Keeping your yard clean? Sharing something from your garden? Pray that your everyday actions are influencing someone for good.

Wednesday
Think of individuals who consistently influenced you positively without preaching with words. Thank God for all the good examples in your life.

Thursday
Dorcas is being remembered for her kindness. What would you like people to remember about you? Pray that your actions please God, even if those you serve are not satisfied.

Friday
Think about these other lines from "Sermons We See":

> I'd rather see a sermon than hear one any day;
> I'd rather one should walk with me than merely tell the way.
> The eye's a better pupil and more willing than the ear,
> Fine counsel is confusing, but example's always clear;
> And the best of all the preachers are the men who live their creeds,
> For to see good put in action is what everybody needs.

Saturday
The last verse of Hopps's hymn is a fitting prayer for the living sermon:

> May I do the good I know, serving gladly here below;
> Then at last go home to Thee, evermore Thine own to be.
> Amen.

CUPFUL #26

HARVEST TIME

> You will be like the wheat that grows until harvest time. Yes, you will live to a ripe old age.
>
> (Job 5:26)

Charles Haddon Spurgeon told a parable about the end of life. Death, he said, visited two old men. He said to one, "It's time to die." The man called his doctor, promising, "I'll give you all my wealth in return for my good health." His doctor could not help, neither could any of the several others he tried. Eventually, Death bound the hands and feet of the old man and took him captive.

Death spoke to the second man, "It's time to die." This man smiled. "I know that you're God's servant whom He sent. I'm ready." Death told him that those who were afraid of him only looked at his hands. He showed the man his entire body and it was the body of an angel, complete with cherub wings. Death put his hand on the man's pulse, and it felt like an affectionate pinch from a loving parent.

Will we fight death like an enemy coming to capture us? Or will we smilingly receive him like God's angel sent to harvest us from the field?

The words of Job 5:26 are among the encouraging truths Job heard from his friends. They compared the righteous to wheat that endured all the hazards of the field—the worms, the drought, the mildew, and the winds—to become ripe for harvest. Death is the designated agent in the harvesting process.

Nothing in this world is worth more than the physical presence of God or the crown of life promised to those who persevere. What will be our focus when Death comes calling? Fighting will not do any good. We would be better off being ready to answer God's call with a smile.

PRAYER: Thank You, God, for life on earth, and for the more precious gift of life in heaven with You. In Jesus' name, Amen.

This Week's Prayer Guide

Sunday
"My home is in Heaven. I'm just traveling through this world" (Billy Graham).

Monday
Revelation 14:13 says, "Blessed are the dead who die in the Lord from now on. 'Yes,' says the Spirit, 'they will rest from their labor, for their deeds will follow them'" (NIV). Live and pray to "die in the Lord" so that after your rest in the grave, eternal life will be your reward.

Tuesday
Rest is important to older folk who, like wheat in a field, have endured until harvest time. Like wheat, their life's task is to mature and produce grain. Ripe grain is part of their purpose. Pray to produce the grain—the character, the influence, the virtues— that God expects of you.

Wednesday
What a blessing it is to live to a ripe old age! You will experience several exciting stages of life, learn many lessons, and enjoy many good fellowships. Pray to leave memories that will inspire gratitude and praise to God in those who follow after you.

Thursday
Eternal life after death is made possible by Christ's sacrificial death on Calvary. He died that we might escape eternal death, and instead live eternally with Him. Pray that our lives show gratitude for His salvation.

Friday
E. E. Hewitt captured the joy of eternal life in "When We All Get to Heaven":

> Sing the wondrous love of Jesus, sing His mercy and His grace;
> In the mansions bright and blessed, He'll prepare for us a place.
> Refrain:
> When we all get to heaven, what a day of rejoicing that will be!
> When we all see Jesus, we'll sing and shout the victory!

Saturday
The longer you live, the more you'll think about Heaven! Thank God for the prospect of a reunion with Jesus and loved ones.

LEAVE IT THERE

BY CHARLES A. TINDLEY

If the world from you withhold of its silver and its gold,
And you have to get along with meager fare,
Just remember, in His Word, how He feeds the little bird,
Take your burden to the Lord and leave it there.

(Chorus)
Leave it there, leave it there,
Take your burden to the Lord and leave it there.
If you trust and never doubt, He will surely bring you out.
Take your burden to the Lord and leave it there.

If your body suffers pain and your health you can't regain,
And your soul is almost sinking in despair,
Jesus knows the pain you feel, He can save and He can heal,
Take your burden to the Lord and leave it there.

When your youthful days are gone and old age is stealing on,
And your body bends beneath the weight of care,
He will never leave you then, He'll go with you to the end,
Take your burden to the Lord and leave it there.

Section Three
HOPE

"But then I think about this, and I have hope: We are still alive because the Lord's faithful love never ends."

(Lamentations 3:21–22)

"Hope is nothing else than the expectation of the things that faith has believed to be truly promised by God. Thus, Faith believes God to be truthful: Hope expects that He will show His veracity at the opportune time."

"Faith is the foundation on which Hope rests; Hope nourishes and maintains Faith."

(Calvin, 1537)

CUPFUL #27

MORE AND MORE HOPE

> I pray that the God who gives hope will fill you with much joy and peace as you trust in him. Then you will have more and more hope, and it will flow out of you by the power of the Holy Spirit.
>
> (Romans 15:13)

Hope, the "confident expectation of eternal salvation" (1 Cor 13:13, AMP) is the support for our purpose, faith, love. If we stop hoping, none of these virtues will function. It is God's Holy Spirit who initiates and maintains our hope.

Emily Dickinson compares hope to a bird that lives inside the human spirit and sings an endless tune:

"Hope" is the thing with feathers –
That perches in the soul –
'And sings the tune without the words –
And never stops – at all –

And sweetest – in the Gale – is heard –
And sore must be the storm –
That could abash the little Bird
That kept so many warm –

I've heard it in the chillest land –
And on the strangest Sea –
Yet – never – in Extremity –
It asked a crumb – of me.

It encourages us when things are bad and it keeps us cheerful when things are good. The severest storm may threaten the bird, but the song does not stop. Think of the Holy Spirit maintaining our hope like the bird maintains the song.

Know, however, that it is ours to choose whether we allow the Holy Spirit to nurture our hope, or let despair sap our spiritual and mental energy. From years of experience, we know how much brighter life seems, how much stronger we feel, how much deeper our joy when we choose hope and remain in fellowship with the Spirit. More Spirit, more hope.

Motivators say that it takes the same amount of energy to worry about the worst as it does to hope for the best. Why not use our energy to maintain our connection with the Spirit, who maintains our hope? By choosing to hope, we ward off the sense of helplessness and uselessness. We survive the pitfalls of depression and despair. We learn from the mistakes we made, and we rejoice at the many others we did not make.

Revelation 21:3–4 describes our ultimate hope: "Now God's home is with people. He will live with them. They will be his people. God himself will be with them and will be their God. He will wipe away every tear from their eyes … All the old ways are gone."

Have you found that your desire for heaven becomes stronger in your old age? Good! Because it should.

PRAYER: Thank You, Heavenly Father, for the gift of hope. May we never give it up. May we allow it to guide us to our eternal home. We pray in Jesus' name, Amen.

This Week's Prayer Guide

Sunday
"Our Christian hope is that we are going to live with Christ ... where life is what it was always meant to be" (Timothy Keller).

Monday
Our Scripture verse says that God gives hope. It adds that it will flow out of you by the power of the Holy Spirit. Pray that hope flows through you daily, so that you can spread it among the folks around you.

Tuesday
The Scripture verse also says that besides hope, God gives joy and peace. Think about how these three virtues enrich your life. Pray for the opportunity to demonstrate them in your interaction with others.

Wednesday
Read the second paragraph of the poem again, and image the songbird singing inside you every minute of the day. Pray that you will keep a song in your heart to keep you cheerful and hopeful. That's good for your physical, mental, and spiritual health.

Thursday
Your primary hope is "Heaven at Last," as expressed in the song by Horatius Bonar:

Angel voices sweetly singing, echoes thro' the blue dome ringing,
News of wondrous gladness bringing; Ah, 'tis heav'n at last!
Refrain:
"Heav'n at last, heav'n at last; O, the joyful story of heav'n at last!
Heav'n at last, heav'n at last; Endless, boundless glory,
In heav'n at last."

Friday

Meditate on, or sing another stanza of "Heaven at Last":

Christ, himself, the living splendor, Christ the sunlight, mild and tender;
Praises to the Lamb we render; Ah, 'tis heav'n at last!

Saturday

Pray again to be peaceful, joyful, and hopeful every day.

CUPFUL #28

THE PURPOSE OF THE WIND

> After Peter and Jesus were in the boat,
> the wind stopped.
> (Matthew 14:32)

We cannot downplay the seriousness of the coronavirus or any other infectious disease that threatens our lives. Neither can we promote a cure solely by spiritual exercises. We adhere to health guidelines and preventative measures while we pray for God's intervention.

These deadly viruses remind us of the wind in the story of Peter walking on the water. The waves threatened him, but the real danger was the strong wind (see Matt. 14:22–33). According to the National Ocean Service, it is the combination of the speed, duration, and fetch (distance traveled) of the wind, that determines the height of the waves.

Like the wind, these sicknesses seem to come out of nowhere. Their speed and fetch are phenomenal. The prospect of their duration is frightening. They cause waves of worry, ill health, confinement, and loss of life. Yet judging from history, winds have limits. The wind in

Peter's story stopped when he and Jesus climbed into the boat. So was the purpose of the wind completed when Peter abandoned his human frailty for the omnipotence of God's divinity?

Could part of the purpose of these health threats be to humble us? To remind us that some things are beyond our control? Perhaps, as in Peter's situation, they may also motivate worship in those who experience or witness miraculous recovery from suffering.

Trust God to control the winds of suffering. Do not focus on their limited strength, but on God's ability to control them. May our love for Him and for each other increase during these crises. May these winds also extract worship from the living and the dying. And may the survivors become wiser and kinder.

> **Like the wind, these sicknesses seem to come out of nowhere. Their speed and fetch are phenomenal.**

PRAYER: Father, we thank You for life and love. We trust You to protect and save us from (or in) all things harmful, now and forever. In Jesus name, Amen.

This Week's Prayer Guide

Sunday
"When we long for life without difficulties, remind us that oaks grow strong in contrary winds" (Peter Marshall).

Monday
Our enemy tries to frighten us, but He cannot touch us without God's permission. Pray to remain close to Jesus—to abide in Him always.

Tuesday
God watches over us, but we must do what we can for our physical well-being. Pray for the discipline to adopt healthy eating and proper hygiene.

Wednesday
What wind is threatening to blow you away today? Aches and pains? Bad news? Bills more than you can pay? Ask Jesus to give you the right approach toward the problem, or to send the right person to help you.

Thursday
God has brought you through storms in the past. Thank Him. Renew your belief that what He has done in the past, He can do again.

Friday
Remember that beautiful song "Peace! Be Still!" by Mary Ann Baker? Meditate on the refrain:

> The winds and the waves shall obey thy will. "Peace, be still!"
> Whether the wrath of the storm-tossed sea,
> Or struggles or evil, whatever it be,
> No water can swallow the ship where lies
> the Master of ocean and earth and skies:
> They all shall sweetly obey thy will.
> "Peace, be still! Peace, be still!"
> They all shall sweetly obey thy will.
> "Peace, peace, be still!"

Saturday
Celebrate God for the victories He has won for you in the past, and for those He's arranging right now. Thank Him profusely!

CUPFUL #29

BE BRAVE

> In this world you will have troubles. But be brave! I have defeated the world!
>
> (John 16:33)

Moses got himself and the children of Israel into trouble even though he did what God told him to do: that is, ask Pharaoh to let the Israelites go. Pharaoh responded by making their tasks more difficult. Instead of granting them a blessing, it seemed that Moses had brought them a greater burden (see Exod. 5: 22–23). But he continued to follow God's lead, and eventually became the deliverer of the Hebrew nation.

If following God ever gets us into trouble, we must also take Him at His word, and be brave. John Lewis, the American politician and social activist who died in 2020 at the age of eighty, will be remembered for his strange advice, "Find a way to get into trouble. Good trouble. Necessary trouble." Following his conscience, he was arrested at least forty-five times for getting into trouble to right social wrongs. An outstanding result of his troubles is the legal end of racial segregation in America.

Perhaps, in our senior years, we may get into trouble when we "speak up for those who cannot speak for themselves; ensure justice for those being crushed" (Prov. 31:8, NLT). "Remember also those being mistreated" (Heb. 13:3, NLT). We may even get into trouble when we rule out "silly stories that don't agree with God's truth" (1 Tim. 4:7). We may initiate trouble–good, necessary trouble, which comes from simply following God's instructions. Let's be brave (but respectful, kind, and gentle) when we need to be.

"Good trouble" is not necessarily a one-man show. Instead of complaining to each other, we can stand together, pray together, and insist on being heard. Let's seek the wisdom and courage of our Heavenly Father who is "our ever-present help in trouble" (Ps. 46:1). The result of our good troubles could be the extension of His kingdom (Matt. 25:40).

> **Perhaps, in our senior years, we may get into trouble when we "speak up for those who cannot speak for themselves; ensure justice for those being crushed" (Prov. 31:8, NLT).**

PRAYER: Dear God, thank You for the opportunity to become vessels through whom You can right wrongs and help the world to live by Your standard of love. In Jesus' name, Amen.

This Week's Prayer Guide

Sunday
"Do not ask for fears to be removed; ask for courage equal to the fears" (Jack Hyles).

Monday
Moses got into trouble with Pharaoh. It was good trouble because he was obeying God. Pray for bravery to do what God says, no matter what.

Tuesday
Think of situations in which you need to be brave in your family, in the church, in dealing with your neighbors. Pray to accept that God has already defeated the world. Ask Him what to do, and pray to be brave.

Wednesday
Has anyone ever gotten into good trouble by standing up for you, when you were not brave enough to stand up for yourself? Thank God for the help, and if it is still possible, express gratitude to that person.

Thursday
Now it's your turn to be brave in standing up (not only physically) for others. Whatever you do for those who need help, you do for Christ. Pray for compassion to be ready to stand up for others.

Friday
You will also have to stand up for Christ. Jesus promised to send a helper. This helper is the Holy Spirit sent by the Father (John 14:26). Pray for a close relationship with the Spirit, so you will be able to recognize and understand Him.

Saturday
Consider these words from the hymn "Stand Like the Brave" by Fanny J. Crosby:

Be Brave

Christian, awake! 'tis the Master's command;
With helmet and shield, and a sword in thy hand,
To meet the bold tempter, go, fearlessly go,
Then stand like the brave, with thy face to the foe.

Refrain
Stand like the brave, stand like the brave,
Stand like the brave, with thy face to the foe.

CUPFUL #30

MONEY

> Keep your lives free from the love of money.
> And be satisfied with what you have. God has said,
> "I will never leave you."
>
> (HEBREWS 13:5)

When I received legal notice that I was single again, I was unemployed. Partially disabled because of a recent accident, I had no idea when I would work again. Away from close relatives, and without financial stability, I felt forsaken.

Despair set in and the enemy of my soul drew near to feed my fear. When I looked at the evening news featuring the helpless and the homeless, he whispered, "That's where you're headed." Then God reminded me of His promise that He would never leave me the way human companions do.

The real estate agent who helped me search for a home to rent was surprised when the owner chose me for a tenant, above couples who were more qualified financially. He had met me, the owner told the agent, and something about me impressed him. That "something about me" influenced him more than money. Might it have been God's providence and protection over me?

This recognition of God's perpetual presence with us is the reason we can be grateful, cheerful, and hopeful even when money is not enough. Having previously experienced His provision when our earnings came up short, when unexpected debt occurred, when the reward that we deserved went to someone else, old folks know about trusting in God to supply their needs.

People, including your children, watch to see how you brave the challenges of aging. Don't give the impression that your hope and satisfaction depend on how much money you have. Show them that money helps, but that it can never mean more to you than the assurance that God is always with you.

PRAYER: Thank You, Heavenly Father, for being always present with us. Thank You for convincing us so that we may convince others, that to have You is to have all that we need. In Jesus' name, Amen.

This Week's Prayer Guide

Sunday
"The fellow that has no money is poor. The fellow that has nothing but money is poorer still" (Billy Sunday).

Monday
"Be satisfied with what you have," says our Scripture verse from Hebrews. Psalm 84:11 states, "The Lord freely gives every good thing to those who do what is right." Pray for faith to accept that God arranges what is best for you.

Tuesday
God promises that He will never leave you. Pray for mindfulness to recognize Him and communicate with Him throughout the day.

Wednesday
Sometimes, instead of money, God sends you the thing you planned to buy with the money. Pray that He opens your eyes to see His provision. Thank Him.

Thursday
Which would you prefer? Twice the money you have? Or twice the knowledge and understanding you have of God's promises? Pray for deeper intimacy between Him and you.

Friday
Sing or meditate on Rhea F. Miller's hymn "I'd Rather Have Jesus":

> I'd rather have Jesus than silver or gold;
> I'd rather be His than have riches untold;
> I'd rather have Jesus than houses or lands.
> I'd rather be led by His nail pierced hand.
>
> Chorus:
> Than to be the king of a vast domain
> Or be held in sin's dread sway.
> I'd rather have Jesus than anything
> This world affords today.

Saturday
Thank God for the peace and joy that comes with contentment.

CUPFUL #31

BE READY ALWAYS

> So be ready all the time. Pray that you will be able to get through all these things that will happen and stand safe before the Son of Man.
>
> (Luke 21:36)

When my daughter was a toddler, she was ready to leave the house as soon as she got dressed. We had to hide her shoes until we were actually ready to walk through the door. She had not yet learned the concept of patience. For her, there were no pauses between ready, set, go.

Jesus wants us to be ready now, and to stay ready until He comes to take His faithful followers away from this sinful world. It's the pause while we wait to go with Him, that tests our maturity. Like my little girl, we may become impatient. We may fuss that the wait is too long. We face the danger of soiling our righteous characters, taking off our gospel shoes, and even falling into a spiritual snooze, frustrated that He has not yet come. "So be ready all the time," He warns.

In the King James version, His words are "Watch … and pray." During the pause, while we wait for Him, there are political upheavals, pandemics, and natural disasters of all sorts. Through it all, He encourages us to watch: to focus on keeping our fellowship with Him intact, to pray for His strength and His grace to help us endure. This is the time for us to encourage each other, to help others practice heavenly behavior.

> **During the pause, while we wait for Him, there are political upheavals, pandemics, and natural disasters of all sorts.**

He expects our mood to be joyful. "When these things begin to happen, stand up tall and don't be afraid. Know that it is almost time for God to free you!" (Luke 21:28). Be ready to be freed from the discomforts of aging, from the uncertainties of pending disasters, from the effects of sin. Be ready for the comforts of our heavenly home and the presence of our Loving Lord. Be ready to go!

PRAYER: Dear Lord, we appreciate life on this earth, and we want to stay ready for eternal life with You, in Heaven. In Jesus' name, Amen.

This Week's Prayer Guide

Sunday
"The Second Coming of Christ … is the only ray of hope that shines as an ever-brightening beam in a darkening world." (Billy Graham)

Monday
On a scale of one to ten, with one measuring least ready and ten measuring most ready, where would you place yourself? Where do you think God would place you? Pray for God to search you and show you any changes you need to make, in order to be ready for His coming.

Tuesday
Pray to be so in love with Jesus that when you think of His second coming, you think joyfully of spending time with Him.

Wednesday
Who are the specific persons you would like to be together with you and Jesus in heaven? Pray for them now to be ready, and for God to show you how you can help them remain ready.

Thursday
While you wait for Jesus to come, does your life manifest the fruit of the Spirit (love, joy, peace, patience, kindness, goodness, faithfulness, gentleness, and self-control)? (See Galatians 5: 22–23). Pray to influence folks around you to be ready for eternal life with Christ.

Friday
"Come, Thou Long–Expected Jesus" is one of Charles Wesley's hymns; it expresses His desire for Jesus to come.

> Come, thou long-expected Jesus born to set thy people free;
> From our fears and sins release us, let us find our rest in thee.
> Israel's strength and consolation, hope of all the earth thou art;
> Dear desire of every nation, joy of every longing heart.

Saturday
Pray to remain ready, patient, and joyful until Jesus comes, or until He calls you to rest while you wait.

CUPFUL #32

THE DEATH OF SAINTS

> Precious in the sight of the Lord
> is the death of his saints.
>
> (PSALM 116:15)

For two hours, the three of us—Death, my mother, and I—shared the room. God was there, too. He assisted me in making peace with the intruder.

My mother had been blessed with eighty-five years of productive life. I had watched her mature from a shy, teenage mother to a mature, influential woman of faith. She worked hard. Now that her brain power had deserted her and her illness had become too stressful for her body, rest seemed like a fitting reward.

I neglected to thank Death, but he had been a relief to my mother. He rescued her from the mental confusion that frustrated her, and the physical pain that her immobile body couldn't escape. Death had been a relief to me also, freeing me from the anguish of watching her become less than human. Moreover, Death was God's agent sent to close out an expired life—a life that was precious to Him.

At her funeral, we sang the hymn "Come, Ye Disconsolate" written in 1816 by Thomas Moore, to the melody arranged in 1831 by Thomas Hastings. It was the tune she hummed most often when she could not remember the other songs she used to know. It contains the following lines, each one at the end of a stanza.

> Earth has no sorrow that heav'n cannot heal.
> Earth has no sorrow that heav'n cannot cure.
> Earth has no sorrow but heav'n can remove.

Death is precious to God when a person dies with the hope of the resurrection. It is precious to Him when that person is a candidate for the choir that will sing the song of victory over death and sin. It is precious to Him because it is the bridge we cross over to spend eternity with Him.

PRAYER: Thank You, God, for the hope of eternal life, which is given to us by Jesus Christ when we accept Him as our Lord and Savior. In Jesus' name, Amen.

This Week's Prayer Guide

Sunday
"Death may be the King of terrors... but Jesus is the King of kings!" (Dwight L. Moody)

Monday
Rest is a deserved reward for someone who has worked hard. The rest period between mortality and immortality is called death. Pray to be at peace when God offers you that rest.

Tuesday
Because you don't know when your rest will begin, it is advisable to be prepared. Making a will, sharing information your loved ones will need, and so on, will be helpful. Pray for

the courage to set your house in order while you still have the time.

Wednesday
As my mother neared death, she said that she heard a choir of angels singing, and she tried to sing along. An angel told her that it was her turn to listen, and soon it would be her turn to sing. She waited patiently. Pray to live in communion with God, so you will die in communion with Him.

Thursday
Imagine God smiling when it is your turn to die, because your death is precious to Him. Pray to die satisfied that your life pleased God.

Friday
Jesus has already conquered death. Pray to be on His side now, so you can be on His side at the resurrection and share with Him the victory over sin and death.

Saturday
Sing or meditate and cheer yourself on with Bessie Doolittle's lyrics in "How Cheering Is the Christian's Hope":

> How cheering is the Christian's hope, while toiling here below!
> It buoys us up while passing thro' this wilderness of woe.
>
> Verse 2
> It points to us a land of rest, where saints with Christ will reign,
> Where we shall meet the loved of earth, and never part again.

CUPFUL #33

GOD'S SMILE

God, accept us again. Smile down on us and save us!
(PSALM 80:3)

We begin a new journey when the new day starts,
Yesterday's steps recede as night departs.
We face today with the understanding
That brand new challenges may be pending.
We engage in devotion and meditation,
We give You the control of our situation,
And it boosts our faith if just for a while,
We envision Your fatherly face with a smile.

As the day progresses and our work takes its toll,
We input our influence on history's scroll.
We try to lift the burdens of others,
Regardless whether they're foes or brothers.
We do what we can and we hope that we're right,
But we make errors, some are plain oversight.
It helps to prevent us from feeling vile
If we know You watch over us with a smile.

And when the day ends and the time comes to retire
From the hustle and bustle of labor for hire,

We may rest and reflect on the impact we made,
And wonder if we caused Your smile to fade.
The words that we've spoken, and the deeds we've done
Have been assessed and to eternity gone.
We trust in Your grace, and pray all the while,
That we gain Your blessing and Your smile.

—Dora Isaac Weithers

PRAYER: Thank You, Father, for encouraging us with Your caring smile of encouragement and approval throughout the day. In Jesus' name, Amen.

This Week's Prayer Guide

Sunday
"God smiles on us when we find something we thought we'd lost." (Maureen Pratt)

Monday
What the King James Version translates as *God's face shining upon you* (see Num. 6:25), the newer versions refer to as *His smile*. Pray to enjoy the benefit of a loving, caring God who also smiles.

Tuesday
In Psalm 80, the psalmist begs God three times to *smile down on us and save us* from suffering in the midst of a disaster. What reason do you have for wanting to see His smile today? Pray that prayer.

Wednesday
Do you imagine God really smiling when you find something you thought you had lost? Reflect on some instances when you can imagine that He smiled, and thank Him.

Thursday
Do you think God smiles when we express a longing for Him? Pray a prayer now that makes Him smile.

Friday
Consider Paul's testimony to his Philippian children in the faith, and pray that you can honestly say the same to those who look to you for an example:

> I know that I still have a long way to go. But there is one thing I do: I forget what is in the past and try as hard as I can to reach the goal before me. I keep running hard toward the finish line to get the prize that is mine because God has called me through Christ Jesus to life up there in heaven . . . join together in following my example (Phil. 3:13–14, 17).

Saturday
Make an effort today to make someone smile. Say something, do something or even provide something for which God will give His approval and His smile.

CUPFUL #34

WHEN YOU NEED HELP

> The Lord's angel came to him again, touched him, and said, "Get up and eat!" ... So Elijah got up. He ate and drank and felt strong.
>
> (1 Kings 19:7–8)

Even spiritual giants like the prophet Elijah are subject to depression. He had recently prayed down fire from heaven and convinced the Israelites to give up their idol worship for worship of Jehovah, the true God. He destroyed the prophets of Baal. But when Jezebel threated to kill him, Elijah lost his courage and ran for his life (see I Kings 18:36–40).

Scared, and feeling hopeless, Elijah lay under a tree in the desert and prayed to die. His spirituality was intact, but his human strength was exhausted. The weight of the problem became more than he could bear—by himself. The promise in Psalm 91:11 came true for him— "He will command his angels to protect you wherever you go." Good reason to feed on God's Word when the mind is clear.

God's angel brought food, from which Elijah ate twice before he was ready to move. It was important for him to eat, to regain physical strength, to support his nervous system and eventually function again. Angels also come in the form of friends, neighbors, relatives, sometimes strangers, who recognize depression.

Depression can be triggered by memories of lost loved ones, or worry over loved ones who are living carelessly. It shows itself in sadness, withdrawal, grumpiness, irritability, and other negative moods. None of this means that you've lost your relationship with God. You just need help to see and hear Him clearly.

When life seems dark, reach out for mental and emotional support from a wise Christian friend or a counseling professional. You may be old and tired, but God has purpose in keeping you. Get up when you can. Eat, drink, follow the doctor's orders and trust God for His strength, as He completes what He started in you.

> **When life seems dark, reach out for mental and emotional support from a wise Christian friend or a counseling professional.**

PRAYER: Father, we trust You to restore us spiritually, mentally and completely whenever we become exhausted. We thank you in Jesus' name, Amen.

This Week's Prayer Guide

Sunday
"There are times when the best thing to do with our feelings is to challenge them: 'Why are you cast down, O my soul, and why are you in turmoil within me? Hope in God; for I shall again praise Him, my salvation and my God' (Ps. 42:11)." (Derek W. H. Thomas)

Monday
Talk to God about feelings you don't share with anyone else. Be sure to include feelings of guilt. Thank Him for the joy of being forgiven.

Tuesday
Cheer yourself up with some lusty singing, before you pray, thanking God for His joy, His peace, and His love.

Wednesday
Pray that someone you know, who often seems sad, might find joy.

Thursday
Pray that God will give you the right words to say if you ever need to encourage someone who is depressed.

Friday
"Does Jesus Care," written by Frank E. Graeff reminds us that Jesus knows and cares about our feelings of grief and sadness:

> "Does Jesus care when my heart is pained
> Too deeply for mirth or song;
> As the burdens press, and the cares distress,
> And the way grows weary and long?
>
> Refrain
> "Oh, yes, He cares; I know He cares, His heart is touched with my grief;
> When the days are weary, the long nights dreary, I know my Savior cares.
>
> Verse #2
> "Does Jesus care when my way is dark
> With a nameless dread and fear?
> As the daylight fades into deep night shades,
> Does He care enough to be near?"

Saturday
Read the Sunday quotation again today, and pray for a spirit of continual praise.

CUPFUL #35

A LEGACY OF KINDNESS

> People who are kind will be rewarded
> for their kindness.
>
> (PROVERBS 17:6)

One of the board members of the Caribbean school to which I was assigned showed me exceptional kindness. He dropped by regularly with gifts of fruits and vegetables, and always inquired about my well-being.

After two years, my assignment ended, and during my farewell event, he approached me. "I've been meaning to ask you whether you're related to someone I used to know." I listened. "When I was a teenager, my youth group visited a youth group on your island. One young man was extremely kind to me. We became friends and made plans for him to visit me. I intended to repay his kindness, but he died before I got the chance."

I told him that I knew the man he was talking about. He sighed, "I am sorry that I never got the chance to return his kindness."

"But you did," I assured him. "You returned it to his daughter."

My father died before I was old enough to remember him, but in that moment when I realized what an impact his kindness had made, and how it had benefitted me, my heart embraced him with all the strength it had. His legacy of kindness affirmed him to be the lovable, desirable, worthy man that God had given me for a father.

Fathers and mothers, what will your children reap from the seeds you have sown? It is not too late to put some kind deeds into the ground where you recognize a need. With God's blessing, the smallest seed will produce fruit. Along with every other good inheritance, may parents leave for their children a legacy of faith and kindness!

PRAYER: Heavenly Father, thank You for all the human fathers who have left legacies of faith and kindness for their children. May their children do the same for the next generation. In Jesus' name, Amen.

This Week's Prayer Guide

Sunday
"If you want to be holy, be kind." (Frederick Buechner)

Monday
Is there a person or persons you will always remember as being kind? If possible, it would be kind to let them know. Give thanks to God for having their lives touch yours.

Tuesday

You can be kind and not be a Christian, but you cannot be a Christian and not be kind. Pray that your kindness is evident when you aim to represent Christ, which should be always.

Wednesday

You are not being kind just so that folks can remember your kindness. Kindness has been put inside you by the Holy Spirit, making it part of your nature, in the same way it was part of Christ's. Pray that the fruit of the Spirit—love, joy, peace, patience, kindness, goodness, faithfulness, gentleness, and self-control (Gal. 5:22–23) will be evident in your life.

Thursday

Your model of kindness is God Himself. Pray for Him to guide you in all your efforts to be kind. Thank Him for giving you something to share.

Friday

Sing or meditate on these two verses from "There's a Wideness in God's Mercy" by Frederick William Faber:

> There's a wideness in God's mercy, like the wideness of the sea.
> There's a kindness in God's justice, which is more than liberty.

> Verse #2
> For the love of God is broader than the measures of the mind,
> And the heart of the Eternal is most wonderfully kind.

Saturday

The greatest reward for your kindness is the gift of eternal life. Thank God for the reunion you will enjoy with others who accepted God's kindness to mankind.

CUPFUL #36

GOD'S EXPECTATIONS

> Zacchaeus was too short... He climbed a sycamore tree... Jesus said, "Zacchaeus, hurry! Come down! I must stay at your house today."
>
> (LUKE 19:3–5)

He was not responsible for his shortness, but he allowed it to influence his expectations. He thought that if only he could get a view of Jesus without any obstruction, that would be a great achievement. So he set out to see Him.

His short legs began to run, and on reaching the sycamore tree, they climbed. His efforts paid off when he saw Jesus from the treetop. He looked at the Master Teacher as if he, Zacchaeus, were a commoner looking at a celebrity in a parade.

The tree gave Zacchaeus a physical and social advantage, but it was just a prop to compensate for his limitation. He was still short in stature and integrity, and Jesus wanted more for Him. "Come down (to earth)" Jesus told Him. Zacchaeus must be his real self if he wanted the maximum benefit of his encounter with Jesus.

Imagine Zacchaeus's surprise when Jesus saw him, called his name, and invited Himself to the short man's house! Zacchaeus gained height in morality and spirituality (verse 8). The haters were furious, because what happened was beyond their expectation.

This may be a good time to determine what you really want. Are you satisfied with pretending that you are in genuine fellowship with Jesus, without being authentic? Or do you want to come down from your prop and let Him free you to allow God's Holy Spirit inside you?

It is never too late to embrace Jesus as the Lord of your life, remembering that "with God's power working in us, he can do much, much more than anything we can ask or think" (Eph. 3:20). Your human expectations may be limited by what you think can happen. God's expectations are governed by His ability to make things happen.

PRAYER: Dear God, today, we raise our expectations and accept the sweet, everlasting fellowship You intend to have with us. In Jesus' name, Amen.

This Week's Prayer Guide

Sunday
"Our God has boundless resources. The only limit is in us. Our expectations are too limited." (A. B. Simpson)

Monday
Jesus wanted more for Zacchaeus than Zacchaeus wanted. Is that how it is with you? Pray to take full advantage of God's resources.

Tuesday
When Jesus went to Zacchaeus' house, Zacchaeus came clean about his wrongdoings and he repented. Are you afraid that getting too close to Jesus will cause you to give

up something you don't want to? Ask God to search your heart and guide you into honest prayer.

Wednesday
Do you realize that even now in your later years, God can bless you and use you beyond your expectations? He can even fulfill a dream you let die many years ago. Pray for willingness to let Him use you.

Thursday
Pray for faith to believe that your history and heredity are powerless to interfere with God's expectations for you.

Friday
The more you love God, the more you will abide in Him Meditate on these words from the hymn "More Love to Thee" by E. Prentiss:

> More love to Thee, O Christ, more love to Thee!
> Hear Thou the prayer I make on bended knee;
> This is my earnest plea: more love, O Christ, to Thee,
> More love to Thee, more love to Thee!
> Verse #2
> Once earthly joy I craved, sought peace and rest;
> Now Thee alone I seek, give what is best;
> This all my prayer shall be: more love, O Christ, to Thee,
> More love to Thee, more love to Thee!

Saturday
Pray that you will learn to give God all the love He expects in return.

CUPFUL #37

TEACHING BY EXAMPLE

> The Recabite family answered, "We never drink wine ... because our ancestor Jonadab son of Recab gave us this command: 'You and your descendants must never drink wine'... So we have obeyed."
>
> (JEREMIAH 35: 5–6, 8)

Jonadab was dead for about three hundred years when God chose his descendants, the Rechabites, to give the Israelites an illustration of obedience. Not even God's prophet could pressure them into disobedience. Meanwhile, the Israelites habitually broke their covenant with God. God instructed Jeremiah to showcase the Rechabites as models of the loyalty and obedience which He expected.

Jonadab's long-standing influence was due to the fact that he taught by example. He demonstrated his own loyalty to the true God in his fight against idolatry, alongside Jehu, who stamped out Baal worship (see 2 Kings 10). He also instructed his descendants to live in tents, so they could easily move away from sacrilegious neighbors who might have surrounded them. He set the example by doing what he told them to do.

When our children are grown and they stray from the path we trained them to follow, we may look back with regret at the behavior we modeled. Perhaps we watched television programs we told them not to watch. Perhaps we neglected to explain certain questionable behaviors, which led them to make false conclusions. Perhaps God is giving us another chance to teach by example.

You can teach humility by admitting that you made some mistakes. You can teach repentance by turning away from old habits and turning toward God's path of righteousness. You can teach surrender by asking Him, in the presence of your children, to forgive and accept you and them.

Your children know when you are serious about something. Tell them again that you would love to see them follow you as you follow God in obedience.

PRAYER: Thank You, Heavenly Father, for forgiving the errors we made in parenting, and for giving us second chances. In Jesus' name, Amen.

This Week's Prayer Guide

Sunday
"Children have never been very good at listening to their elders, but they have never failed to imitate them." (James Baldwin)

Monday
Think of a specific habit or saying that your children have copied from you, that you would like them to pass on to their children. Pray that your offspring remain true to that principle and all the other lessons you taught them.

Tuesday
Think of a specific habit which your parents or parent figures taught you by example more than by words. Thank God for those who left good footprints for you to follow.

Wednesday
Pray that God arranges for your children to learn the good that you neglected to teach. Pray that they do not perpetuate the errors they saw you make. Thank God for His forgiveness.

Thursday
Pray to be mindful of what you are still teaching your children about healthy aging and focusing on heaven.

Friday
As long as you have the opportunity to mentor others in obedience to God, be faithful in your task, so you can say like Paul in his testimony and appeal to those who looked up to him:

> "Brothers and sisters, I know that I still have a long way to go. But there is one thing I do: I forget what is in the past and try as hard as I can to reach the goal before me. I keep running hard toward the finish line to get the prize that is mine because God has called me through Christ Jesus to life up there in heaven. ... Brothers and sisters, join together in following my example"
>
> (Philippians 3:13, 14, 17).

Saturday
Thank God that both you and your children can continue to learn godly living from the example and teachings of Jesus Christ.

CUPFUL #38

A PRAYER FOR WISDOM

> Teach us how short our lives are so that
> we can become wise.
>
> (PSALM 90:12)

The King James Version reads, "Teach us to number our days." The Easy-to-Read Version suggests that when we do, we will conclude that life is short.

Jesus told a parable about a rich man who was quite misguided while numbering his days (see Luke 12:16). Having produced a good crop, he built new barns and saved enough wheat to last him for many years, but he had only one more night. When he numbered his days, selfishness robbed him of the ability to count wisely. He did not make space to include love, kindness, and care for others.

Numbering our days is about being mindful that each day counts. It is about thanking God and asking for His wisdom so that we might fill the day with words and deeds that benefit His Kingdom. It is about reflecting on our blessings, recognizing our shortcomings, correcting our mistakes, and embracing and practicing His forgiveness. It is about making a positive difference every day in the life of someone else. It is about learning from God, through His Word and through our fellowship with Him, how to be wiser today than we were yesterday.

We realize how short our lives are when we number each day as one day less than the days God assigned for us, to do what He planned for us to do—one less day to spend with our loved ones, one less day to pursue the goal we're passionate about, one day nearer to our last breath. This realization prompts us to live every day to the full.

> It is about reflecting on our blessings, recognizing our shortcomings, correcting our mistakes, and embracing and practicing His forgiveness. It is about making a positive difference every day in the life of someone else.

The longer you live, the less time you have for detours, procrastinations, and willful idleness. You do realize how swiftly the days come to an end, and you want to maximize your time with acts of significance. Eternal consequences are on your mind. Nothing you can pray for now, is more important than God's wisdom.

PRAYER: Dear God, please "teach us how short our lives are, so we can become wise." In Jesus' name, Amen.

This Week's Prayer Guide

Sunday
"Instead of calculating our days by any earthly timepiece, may we calculate them by the numbers of opportunities and mercies which are … burning out, never to be relighted." (T. De Witt Talmage)

Monday
Becoming wiser about numbering your days will help you to include God in your plans for each day. Pray that you will learn to allow His input and trust His directions.

Tuesday
Many believers have said that sometimes God changes the plans they make, and that when He does, their day is more productive. Pray to be attentive, going forward. Thank God that He allows His wisdom to override yours, for your own good.

Wednesday
How serious are you about using your time wisely? Be aware that time spent can never be regained. Pray to accept God's control over the time you spend in devotion, in watching television, in chat forums or chatting by phone, and in your God-given tasks.

Thursday
A wise day's schedule will include rest. Pray to practice balance for your spiritual and mental health benefit.

Friday
Reflect on this counsel from Ellen White: "Our time belongs to God. Every moment is His, and we are under the most solemn obligation to improve it to His glory … We have no time to waste, no time to devote to selfish pleasure, no time for the indulgence of sin. It is now that we are to form characters for the future, immortal life" *(Christ's Object Lessons,* p. 342).

Saturday
God wants you to demonstrate wisdom in the way you spend your days. Pray to be a good influence on those who are watching.

CUPFUL #39

A GOOD FUTURE

> This message is from the Lord.
> "I have good plans for you.
> I don't plan to hurt you. I plan to give you
> hope and a good future."
> (Jeremiah 29:11)

Alice, a Christian and retired health professional, set her heart on relocating to another part of the country. She wanted warmer temperatures, which would make it more comfortable for her to continue serving others as a volunteer.

She decided on a certain city, made her plans, and was excited about the move, but at the last moment, those plans fell through. She was disappointed, but not discouraged. She had always believed the promise in Jeremiah 29:11, that God was planning a good future for her.

She restarted her planning, and progressed for the second time, to the point of moving to her city of choice, when her plans fell through again. By now, she realized that God's plan was different from hers.

A long-time friend who had no notion about her efforts to move, called to chat. The friend invited her to move to her city, where the temperature was warmer, and where there was volunteering opportunity in the area of her training.

Not long after, Alice moved. She suffered some health complications that required treatment with a huge cost. Because she volunteered at the health facility, her treatment was free. God's delays had helped, not hurt, her.

Do you realize that God is great enough to plan the details of your future in advance? He is good enough to prevent you from sabotaging His plan for you. He loves you and wants to bless you so that you can bless others. Don't fight Him when He changes your plan. Trust Him and thank Him instead.

PRAYER: Thank You, Our Omniscient God, for keeping Your promise to give us hope and a good future, even in our aging years. In Jesus' name, Amen.

This Week's Prayer Guide

Sunday
"Never be afraid to trust an unknown future to a known God." (Corrie Ten Boom)

Monday
Still hoping for prayers and dreams from the past to come true? Pray today for faith to believe that God's plan for you is still on schedule.

Tuesday
Major disappointments often become major blessings in the future. Pray that even when you feel letdown, your hope in God will remain alive.

Wednesday
Pray that you do not become anxious and run ahead of God; that could sabotage and delay what God is planning for you. Renew your hope in Him every day.

Thursday

Talk with God today about your hope for your children, younger family members, church family, and others you care about. Look for opportunity to share your hope with them. Pray with them too.

Friday

William Cowper's hymn "God Moves in a Mysterious Way" suggests that we cannot always trace the steps by which God bring our hopes to fruition. Meditate on these two verses:

> "God moves in a mysterious way His wonders to perform.
> He plants his footsteps in the sea and rides upon the storm.
>
> Verse #2
> "You fearful saints, fresh courage take; the clouds you so much dread
> Are big with mercy and shall break in blessings on your head."

Saturday

"So, Lord, what hope do I have? You are my hope!" (Psalm 39:7). Pray to accept that having God is having the fulfillment of all your hopes.

JESUS LOVES ME, THIS I KNOW

(SENIOR VERSION – AUTHOR UNKNOWN)

Jesus loves me, this I know,
Though my hair is white as snow.
Though my sight is growing dim,
Still He bids me trust in Him.

(Chorus)
Yes, Jesus loves me; Yes, Jesus loves me;
Yes, Jesus loves me, The Bible tells me so.

Though my steps are oh, so slow,
With my hand in His I'll go
On through life, let come what may,
He'll be there to lead the way.

Though I am no longer young,
I have much which He's begun.
Let me serve Christ with a smile,
Go with others the extra mile.

Jesus Loves Me, This I Know

When the nights are dark and long,
In my heart He puts a song.
Telling me in words so clear,
"Have no fear, for I am near."

When my work on earth is done,
And life's victories have been won.
He will take me home above,
Then I'll understand His love.

Section Four
LOVE

"I pray that your life will be strong in love and be built on love… That … all God's holy people will … understand the greatness of Christ's love —how wide, how long, how high, and how deep that love is."
(Ephesians 3:17–18)

"When Christ's love fills our hearts, it puts selfishness on the run."
(Billy Graham)

"Love is not just reserved for our inner circle… It is intended to be the currency of our world… If you are going to transform your life … to a long list of moments for joy, then you have to learn the secret. The secret is to say in your head to every person you meet, 'I love you and there's nothing you can do about it.'"
(John O'Leary)

"True love is not merely a sentiment or an emotion. It is a living principle, a principle that is manifest in action. True love … will control the life."
(White, *Letters and Manuscripts*, Vol. 15, 1900)

CUPFUL #40

MORE AND MORE LOVE

> This is my prayer for you: that your love will grow
> more and more;
> that you will have knowledge and understanding
> with your love.
>
> (PHILIPPIANS 1:9)

The greatest of all graces is love—"unselfish love for others growing out of God's love for us" (1 Cor. 13:13, AMP).

We may have experienced the joy that comes with loving someone. The more we poured love into that special person, the more the love heaped up inside us. We became happier, felt richer, and got along better with everyone, because love brought out our best attitude and habits. We grew as our love grew.

Later, strong love influenced our decision to share our life with someone. Then children came and we learned to love them unconditionally. We matured still more and loved the grandchildren even when we did not understand them. We cannot stop loving now!

Research shows that without close relationships, we are more susceptible to early death, and more likely to suffer from an emotional or mental disorder. But love keeps us connected and healthier. For stronger love, start with loving God more, making Him the center of your life.

Love Him more passionately through consistent worship. Your fellowship with Him will spill over into a desire for fellowship with others.

Learn from Christ's example—love the rude, the dirty, and the ungrateful. It would be great if they all returned your love, but your main concern is representing God, by loving them in the way He loves you. No matter what else people say, do not make it possible for them to say with any truth that you are not loving. How could you not be loving, when God's constant love for you makes your own love stronger?

PRAYER: Loving Father, may the love that You put within our hearts expand and keep us growing in our love for You and for one another. In Jesus' name, Amen.

This Week's Prayer Guide

Sunday
"Love one another. We don't need more instructions; we need more examples." (Bob Goff)

Monday
God is love. He is the source of love. Because He will never run out of love, neither can you. Pray to understand that, to the point where you are generous, not stingy, with your love.

Tuesday
"If we say we love God but hate any of our brothers or sisters … we are liars" (1 John 4:20). Pray that your love for God will influence you to love people you find difficult to love.

Wednesday
Pray to demonstrate love in every aspect of your life. Acts of courtesy, respect, kindness, hospitality, and other good

deeds are all evidence of love. Pray to love consistently in your interactions with others.

Thursday
"Love at Home" written by John H. McNaughton includes a verse that some may not have seen before. Let it influence your prayer today.

> There's no question you can't ask, when there's love at home;
> There is strength for any task, when there's love at home;
> Sharing joy in work or play, confidence to face the day,
> Knowing love will find a way, when there's love at home.

Friday
When love is in the atmosphere, we become considerate, we forgive offenses, life becomes more manageable. Thank God for the people who usually share (or shared) this kind of atmosphere with you.

Saturday
It is God who makes love possible. Thank Him for His love. Pray that you and your loved ones will never fall out of love with Him.

CUPFUL #41

FORGIVE AND REMEMBER

> Forgive our sins, just as we have forgiven
> those who did wrong to us.
>
> (Matthew 6:12)

In 1995, Azim Khamisa lost his twenty-year-old son to a bullet from fourteen-year-old Tony Hicks. Five years later, Khamisa met his son's killer. In his CBS interview, the father said that he expected to see a killer in Hicks, but instead he saw a soul very much like his own.

Khamisa started corresponding with Hicks and became a surrogate father who promised to be there for the prisoner, who was scheduled to be paroled in 2027. Khamisa's philosophy is that having rescued Tony Hicks with his love, he has given Tony the tools to rescue many others. What a representation of God's love for us who are offered redemption through the death of His Son!

While we may struggle to forget the betrayal, disappointment, and humiliation caused by offenses, we do not want to forget the positive effects of forgiveness, which can empower us to move forward.

Remember that God forgives us continually and abundantly, so we can afford to share His forgiveness generously with others. *Remember* that forgiveness frees us from resentment and hate, which imprison only us, not our offenders. *Remember* that forgiveness grows our resilience and character strengths; it makes us stronger, not weaker, as we move forward. *Remember* that only after we forgive, do we see clearly that what seems like the greatest evil, God can turn into the greatest good (Gen. 50:20).

> **Remember that forgiveness frees us from resentment and hate, which imprison only us, not our offenders.**

Love, joy, and peace of mind do not reside in hearts that are crippled with thoughts of retaliation and revenge. Do yourself a life-giving favor. Let the love from God's Holy Spirit instill in your heart the principles of His forgiveness.

PRAYER: Thank You, Heavenly Father, for the gift of Your forgiveness. Please help us demonstrate our gratitude by sharing this boundless gift with those who offend us. In Jesus' name, Amen.

This Week's Prayer Guide

Sunday
"To be a Christian means to forgive the inexcusable, because God has forgiven the inexcusable in you." (C.S. Lewis)

Monday
We do not appreciate enough what it cost God to forgive us. Pray with thanksgiving for the sacrifice of Christ's death on the cross, which makes forgiveness possible.

Tuesday
Imagine forgiving the person who killed your child. It is difficult, if you leave God out of the picture, but it might

help to *remember* that He also forgave His Son's killers. Pray to learn from Him how to forgive as sincerely as He forgives.

Wednesday
If you do not forgive your offender, you relive the pain whenever you see the person, hear the name, or remember the incident. You become a prisoner to the person who did you wrong. Pray for the grace to forgive and enjoy your freedom.

Thursday
Pray for persons you think might be blaming you for something negative that happened in their lives. Ask God to forgive all the wrongs you have done, and for the courage to apologize and mend broken relationships.

Friday
Consider the truth in Robert Frost's poem "The Star-Splitter." See what happens if everyone refuses to forgive everyone.

> If one by one we counted people out
> For the least sin, it wouldn't take us long
> To get so we had no one left to live with.
> For to be social is to be forgiving.

Saturday
What do you consider the greatest benefit of forgiveness? Thank God for that and for all the other benefits. Pray for all your loved ones to experience it.

CUPFUL #42

BE HAPPY

> Fill us with your love every morning.
> Let us be happy and enjoy our lives.
>
> (PSALM 90:14)

Ella is an individual I always remember. Soon after my roommate and I moved into her neighborhood, she came by to introduce herself. She was a primary-school teacher and a member of the church across the street. We informed her that the absence of living room furniture was our reason for not inviting her in.

"Well, I see plenty of floor space," she said between chuckles, while she gently pushed us aside. She sat down, propping her back against the wall. So did we.

Ella became a frequent visitor to our house, and she always brought laughter. No matter what the mood was when she came in, she left us feeling joyful and energetic. Most of her conversation was about church and work—something funny the pastor said, something one of her students did—and sometimes about her own folly. She also made it clear to us that she had a relationship with Christ.

"How do you manage to be so happy all the time?" I asked her. "Seriously," she offered, "my Christian duty is to spread cheer. I like to make people smile, to see the rainbow in the clouds, to lighten their burdens. That's my purpose."

Upon reflection, I wonder if Ella prayed Psalm 90:14 every day. The verse suggests that we need to be filled with God's love in order to be happy and joyful. Nothing outside of us could bring happiness. Our joy is fueled by God's love inside us.

So how do you experience joy in your life? By being filled with the Spirit, through daily prayer and reading of God's Word. Even when life becomes difficult, His love will surround you and keep your joy intact.

PRAYER: Thank You, loving Father, for the daily filling of Your love, to keep us loving ourselves, and others. In Jesus' name. Amen.

This Week's Prayer Guide

Sunday
"Do you want a happy heart when you are old? Then get with the Lord and stay with Him. That is how it works." (Shelton Smith)

Monday
Our Scripture verse is a prayer that God will fill us with His love. Pray this prayer for yourself and for others you know, by name.

Tuesday
Since God's love in your heart enables you to be happy and enjoy your life, what excuse could you possibly have for being grumpy and miserable? Pray for the courage to confess what makes you unhappy (if you are). Or pray for someone who seems unhappy.

Wednesday
Your happiness makes you kind and pleasant in your dealings with others. Has anyone ever asked you why you are so happy? Ask God for the opportunity to explain how your connection with Him helps to keep you cheerful.

Thursday
Your mood affects the mood of your home, a meeting, or wherever you are. Pray to spread cheer, not gloom, all around you.

Friday
Sing or meditate on these lines from "His Eye Is on the Sparrow" by Civilla D. Martin.

> Why should my heart be lonely, and long for heav'n and home;
> When Jesus is my portion? My constant Friend is he;
> His eye is on the sparrow, and I know he watches me;
> His eye is on the sparrow, and I know he watches me.
> Refrain:
> "I sing because I'm happy, I sing because I'm free;
> For his eye is on the sparrow, And I know he watches me.

Saturday
God loves you and is watching over you. That is reason to be happy. Thank Him.

CUPFUL #43

A PRAYER FOR LOVED ONES

> I want them to be strengthened and joined together with love ... I want them to know completely the secret truth ... That truth is Christ himself.
>
> (COLOSSIANS 2:2)

"Picture a large circle, from the edge of which are many lines all running to the center. The nearer these lines approach the center, the nearer they are to one another. Thus it is in the Christian life. The closer we come to Christ, the nearer we shall be to one another" (White, *Letters and Manuscripts*, Vol. 19, p. 1).

Paul's prayer for the church family is appropriate for the biological family. He prays that they become knitted together by the strong thread of love. If the knitting unravels, the family pattern will be lost, and each member will become a piece of dangling thread, which cannot find its place. To prevent the destruction of the family unity, each member must remain connected to Christ.

Christ embodies the wisdom and knowledge that we need to make sense of life. His principles and promises motivate us to let go of worldly ideas and possessions, which bring temporary thrills. His Word reveals the attitudes and lifestyles that have eternal values. The more closely we follow Him, the more we learn to love Him. The more we love Him, the more we learn to love each other.

The prayers of the elderly are not complete without the prayer for our loved ones to accept Christ's salvation, His eternal life, and everything in between. We want to envision them loving each other, so that disagreements get settled, support develops as a family trademark, and divorces become extinct. In our love for them, may we point them to God, our heavenly Father, the source of all true love.

PRAYER: May our loved ones be strengthened and joined together with love. May each one strive to know and love You completely. In Jesus' name, Amen.

This Week's Prayer Guide

Sunday
"Whatever disunites man from God, also disunites man from man." (Edmund Burke)

Monday
God strengthens and joins the family together in love. Pray for each member of the group to remain connected with God. This makes it easy for all to stay united to each other.

Tuesday
One of the greatest challenges to unity nowadays is family members relocating to distant places. Thank God for the various media platforms and devices by which members can still schedule prayer time together.

Wednesday

How do we maintain fellowship with adult children who have given up the faith and turn their backs on God? Pray for God's Holy Spirit to trouble their consciences. Pray to keep loving them, and trusting God.

Thursday

In some families, disagreements happen more often than not. We can change that. Pray for closer connection with God. Ask for more love, peace, and patience in dealing with each other. Make each other laugh more often.

Friday

Pray that your home, and the homes of your loved ones, will be like the home that Henry Ware described in the first and last stanzas of "Happy the Home When God Is There:"

> Happy the home when God is there,
> And love fills every breast;
> When one their wish, and one their prayer,
> And one their heav'nly rest.

> Lord, let us in our homes agree
> This blessed peace to gain;
> Unite our hearts in love to Thee,
> And love to all will reign.

Saturday

Do you ever think of your family united in heaven with all of God's family? Pray that your family unit will be unbroken. Pray for each member as often as each comes to mind.

CUPFUL #44

BRUISED BUT NOT DESTROYED

We are hurt sometimes, but we are not destroyed.

(2 CORINTHIANS 4:9)

My brass-framed wall clock stopped working. Because of the Bible verse inscribed on it, I did not throw it out. I set it on an easel on a small table in my bedroom, as an attractive non-functional item.

One morning, I accidentally knocked it to the floor where it stayed separated from the battery for the rest of the day. When I decided to put it back together, something incredible happened. It regained life and began to tick. And that's not all. When I tried to reset it, it was showing the correct time. It deserved a best-performance award, not for keeping up, but for catching up.

All of us have been through several types of falls besides the physical. The spiritual and moral falls may be too many to count. The financial and social falls may have left their dents. Each fall halted our progress, but none of them destroyed us. In fact, each fall proved that we were still alive, because we felt the impact.

We are never too old for God to help us up from the falls we have suffered. His omnipotent hand can fix us, if we admit our helplessness and surrender to His restoration. Just like the clock resets to the right time after it has been repaired, so God's grace can restore us to the original function for which He made us. He forgives us for not keeping up, and He enables us to catch up.

You catch up when your bruises remind you of the lessons you learned, when you thank the folks who tested your balance by trying to knock you over, when you move your list of disappointments over to your list of blessings. You may have fallen down. But God helped you get up, stand up, and catch up with the plan He originally designed for you. Why are you not shouting?

> We are never too old for God to help us up from the falls we have suffered.

PRAYER: Gracious God, we thank You that the falls that did not destroy us have strengthened us. Thanks for Your restoration. In Jesus' name, Amen.

This Week's Prayer Guide

Sunday
"When we learn from experience, the scars of sin can lead us to restoration and a renewed intimacy with God." (Charles Stanley)

Monday
Have you ever felt that you missed out on God's blessing because of mistakes you made, or setbacks you encountered? Thank God that He is still in control. Trust Him to get you to the destiny He ordained for you.

Tuesday
Sometimes you trip and fall and the enemy tries to keep you down, but God holds your hand and pulls you up. Thank Him for carrying you on His shoulder when you are too weak or too tired to walk.

Wednesday
Pray that the youth in your family and in your church will look to God and receive His help if they ever fall.

Thursday
Pray for the leaders in your church and community, who trust in God, that they will remain firm at their post.

Friday
Jesus saves, and He restores us when we confess our sins. Thank Him for His forgiveness and restoration.

Saturday
Robert Lowry's song "Nothing but the Blood of Jesus"" gives the perfect remedy for restoration, regardless of the reason for your fall. Sing about it.

> What can wash away my sin? Nothing but the blood of Jesus;
> What can make me whole again? Nothing but the blood of Jesus.
>
> Verse #2
> "This is all my hope and peace—Nothing but the blood of Jesus!
> This is all my righteousness—Nothing but the blood of Jesus!

CUPFUL #45

THINGS WE REMEMBER

> Lord ... I remember the amazing things
> you did long ago.
> I think about those things. I think about
> them all the time.
>
> (Psalm 77:11–12)

There is a story about a woman who never used the offensive F-word. Still, in her old age, when she began to lose control of her mind, she claimed that the word was always on the tip of her tongue. She had grown up with adults who used it constantly, and her brain had stored it away in her long-term memory.

There is another story, of a French army general who had learned the Lord's Prayer in his native language when he was a child. Although he had not prayed it as an adult, he remembered and recited on his death bed.

We are not aware of all the memories, good and bad, which have been stored in our brains. Scientists believe that the memories that are recalled most often, become stronger and easier to remember.

The psalmist Asaph began reflecting on his struggle with God for comfort and assurance. He remembered how upset He was when He thought that God didn't help Him. Then he put effort into remembering the miracles that gave Him hope—God's deliverance of the Hebrews from Egyptian slavery and His control of nature as He led them through the Red Sea. He purposely recalled incidents of God's goodness and solidified them in His mind by writing about them.

What memories do you recall and focus on most often? Remember episodes of God's goodness. Remember the kindness of others. Remember the sweet fellowships you enjoyed. Count your blessings. Add hope and joy to your life and the lives of those around you, by remembering the times that inspired praise to God and admiration for others.

PRAYER: Thank You, Lord, for the memories of Your goodness in our lives. May Your love inspire us to remember with joy. In Jesus' name, Amen.

This Week's Prayer Guide

Sunday
"Remembering with thanks is what causes us to trust—to really believe." (Ann Voskamp)

Monday
Are there some unpleasant thoughts that come to your mind often, which you would rather forget? Pray for the ability to replace those thoughts with positive thoughts about the person or incident. You may have some forgiving to do. Forgive. Thank God that you survived the situation and allow Him to help you move forward.

Tuesday
Have some Bible promises reserved in your memory or in an easy place to find, so you can reach for them when bad memories threaten your joy.

Wednesday
Pray for opportunity to remind someone of the good things God has done for you, for them, or for anyone else.

Thursday
Pray to speak words and perform deeds that others will be happy to remember. Help make some good memories for someone.

Friday
Pray that the greatest act of God's love for you will always be in your memory. To show your gratitude, talk about it as often as possible.

Saturday
Jennie Evelyn Hussey wrote the beloved hymn "Lead Me to Calvary.". Focusing on Christ helps the believer to remember His ultimate act of love.

> "King of my life, I crown Thee now, Thine shall the glory be;
> Lest I forget Thy thorn-crowned brow, lead me to Calvary.
> Chorus:
> Lest I forget Gethsemane; lest I forget Thine agony;
> Lest I forget Thy love for me, lead me to Calvary."

CUPFUL #46

LOVE IS PATIENT

> Love is patient and kind.
>
> (I Corinthians 13:4)

My grandfather's handwriting was horrible—so horrible that it took me several attempts to read it through. He wrote his sweetest letter to me the year I turned twenty-one. I grabbed the foreign money that he always included, read the first paragraph, and then put it down, intending to finish it later.

Days passed, then weeks. Finally, ready to respond to his letter, I read it through and discovered a big surprise. He had invited me to spend Christmas with him. What reason could I possibly have for delaying my response to such a generous offer? I apologized profusely, hoping that he had not changed his mind.

When my grandfather responded, he was as happy as could be, that I agreed to come. No scolding. No mention of my delay. In one sitting, I read that letter through. No horrible handwriting could prevent me from reading through his plans for my visit. In reflection, the happiest times of my stay with him were at breakfast time every morning, when he was most leisurely and most talkative.

The way my grandfather initiated and nurtured the love between us is just like the way God initiates and nurtures our relationship with Him. He reaches out first. He patiently waits for us to repent and respond to Him in obedience. He is not there waiting to slap us on the wrist when we reach for something we shouldn't have. Meanwhile, He keeps on loving us, wanting us to recognize the benefits of His patient, unconditional love.

> **The way my grandfather initiated and nurtured the love between us is just like the way God initiates and nurtures our relationship with Him.**

God loves you with all the love He has, even before you return His love. He loves you even when your response is contrary to what He expects. He waits for you because your space in His heart is reserved for you. What do you think would happen if you were to try loving a difficult person so intentionally? Try it.

PRAYER: Patient, Heavenly Father, please help us practice Your patient love in our relationship with others. We pray with thanksgiving, in Jesus' name. Amen.

This Week's Prayer Guide

Sunday
"The only way love can last a lifetime is if it's unconditional. The truth is this: love is not determined by the one being loved but rather by the one choosing to love." (Stephen Kendrick)

Monday
Has it really sunk in, how much God loves you, even when you do not express love for Him? Thank Him for His amazing, unconditional love.

Tuesday
Pray that in response to His love, you will choose to love Him, and your life will demonstrate your love for Him.

Wednesday
Pray that some specific person(s) you know will recognize God's love, stop turning away from Him, and begin to love Him.

Thursday
If there is broken fellowship between you and someone you care about, pray that God shows you how to initiate the mend. If you have no broken fellowship, thank God.

Friday
Charles Wesley's "And Can It Be, That I Should Gain?" talks about God's amazing love. He loves unconditionally, even when we hurt Him.

> And can it be that I should gain
> An int'rest in the Savior's blood?
> Died He for me, who caused His pain?
> For me, who Him to death pursued?
> Amazing love! How can it be
> That Thou, my God, should die for me?
>
> Refrain:
> Amazing love! how can it be
> That Thou, my God, should die for me!

Saturday
Thank God again that He loves—first, unconditionally, and always.

CUPFUL #47

THE BEAUTY OF KINDNESS

> And the King will say, "I tell you the truth, when you
> did it to one
> of the least of these my brothers and sisters, you were
> doing it to me!"
> (Matthew 25:40 NLT)

Della's aim is to represent Christ by being a model resident in her community. The verse above is always on her mind as she seizes opportunities to minister to the needs of her neighbors. Now that she is retired, she has extra time to cook a few local delicacies that are not often on the home menu, and she distributes them to persons who otherwise might not be privileged to have such good food.

Della's neighbors know her to be a kind Christian woman, and she adds her testimony of God's goodness to her kind deeds. She pays special attention to an adult member of the community who may be considered one of "the least of these," because he is mentally challenged and his language is cluttered. He cares for himself rather poorly and needs help in making a decent appearance. Once, after Della helped him clean up and provided him with a change of clothing, he looked her in the eyes and said, "You look beautiful."

The man's compliment to Della registered on her heart as a commendation from God. Did He not say that an act of kindness to a neighbor is counted as an act of kindness toward Him? It might even be, that through his words, God was speaking to Della's heart, letting her know that her act of kindness revealed the beautiful person she was on the inside.

How many more acts of kindness would you engage in, if you knew that you would receive an audible expression of thanks from God? Even "the least of these" may strive to hear His voice. Think of how much beauty you add to our community by your simple words or deeds of kindness!

PRAYER: Kind Heavenly Father, may we search for an opportunity to represent Your kindness, and cause someone to tell you thanks. In Jesus' name, Amen.

This Week's Prayer Guide

Sunday
"The truth is, we cannot truly be beautiful without kindness." (Natalie Lynn Borton)

Monday
If folks ever stop calling you beautiful, will they stop calling you kind? Pray that especially in your aging years when your facial features change, your beauty will shine in your kindness.

Tuesday
Do you ever find yourself withholding kindness from someone who, in your opinion, does not deserve it? Pray that God will give you the compassion to be kind whenever and to whomever you can.

Wednesday
Do you praise kindness or beauty in the youth around you? Pray to communicate to them that both virtues support each other.

Thursday
Do you ever tell people in your age group that they are beautiful? Pray for the kindness to cheer them up by commending them in areas where they are still beautiful: hair, voice, kindness, encouragement, prayer.

> Do you ever find yourself withholding kindness from someone who, in your opinion, does not deserve it? Pray that God will give you the compassion to be kind whenever and to whomever you can.

Friday
Henry Burton pens the best response to kindness in "Have You Had a Kindness Shown"

> Have you had a kindness shown? Pass it on, pass it on!
> "'Twas not giv'n for thee alone, pass it on, pass it on!
> Let it travel down the years, let it wipe another's tears;
> Till in heav'n the deed appears, pass it on, pass it on!
>
> Refrain:
> "Pass it on, pass it on! Cheerful word or loving deed, pass it on,
> Live for self, you live in vain; Live for Christ, you live again,
> Live for Him, with Him you reign. Pass it on, pass it on!"

Saturday
Pray to leave behind a legacy of kindness, for the benefit of your children and their children.

CUPFUL #48

FELLOWSHIP WITH GOD

> Father to the fatherless, defender of widows—
> this is God, whose dwelling is holy.
>
> (PSALM 68:5)

Imagine strolling or limping or being pushed in a wheelchair across the walkway to a palatial residence. You enter and make yourself comfortable on the sofa. While you are looking around, amazed at all the exquisite furnishings, the host walks over and embraces you. He's God—your God, and He's available to spend one-on-one time with you. While there, you forget about the actual home in which you live alone. You feel revived in His home atmosphere.

We are free to visualize our fellowship with God however we want, but it is more important to experience it. Most elderly individuals have outlived their parents, to become motherless and fatherless. Some outlive their spouses, to become widows and widowers. When we yearn for company, God can transport us into His presence for spiritual fellowship.

We are not downplaying the importance of a human shoulder to lean on, or the closeness of a human embrace. We love having someone sit near us to listen to our stories. We appreciate the caretaker, or the caring relative who stops by to make sure that we're comfortable. We thank

God for their thoughtfulness, but try as they might, they are not always available.

God invites you to enjoy His presence whenever your heart desires. You may connect with Him through prayer, singing, Scripture reading or any activity that puts your focus on Him. When you mourn your loved ones, He comforts you. When you feel afraid, He becomes your protection. Whenever you are conscious of His presence, you experience a home atmosphere. Spiritual fellowship with Him now is a foretaste of being physically at home with Him in Heaven.

PRAYER: Dear God, we thank You for Your presence, for companionship, for comfort, and for all the ways You supply our need. in Jesus' name, Amen.

This Week's Prayer Guide

Sunday
"When a Christian shuns fellowship with other Christians, the devil smiles. When he stops studying the Bible, the devil laughs. When he stops praying, the devil shouts for joy." (Corrie Ten Boom)

Monday
How long do you think you can be all right without fellowship with God? Don't try to find out. Pray that you will always desire His fellowship.

Tuesday
God is always present. Why might you ignore Him? Too much worry? Too much pain? Pray that nothing will distract you from His presence.

Wednesday
You can also experience God's presence in nature study. Pray for the awareness of God's power in His handiwork.

Thursday
What makes heaven attractive to you? Is it freedom from pain or stress, or the fact that you love God? Pray that through your devotional time with Him, you will learn to love Him completely.

Friday
Thank God that salvation from sin and fellowship with God is made possible by Christ's death on the cross for you.

Saturday
"Heaven at Last" is the title of Horatio Bonar's song in which He states that Christ will be the highlight of Heaven.

> Angel voices sweetly singing,
> Echoes thro' the blue dome ringing,
> News of wondrous gladness bringing;
> Ah, 'tis heav'n at last!
>
> Refrain:
> "Christ, himself, the living splendor,
> Christ the sunlight, mild and tender;
> Praises to the Lamb we render;
> Ah, 'tis heav'n at last!

CUPFUL #49

THE SEARCHING SHEPHERD

> Suppose one of you has 100 sheep,
> but one of them gets lost...
> You will continue to search for it until you find it.
>
> (LUKE 15:4)

Many of us who "grew up in the church" as we like to say, do not perceive ourselves as ever having strayed. We participated in every service, never did drugs or attended wild parties, never practiced promiscuity, have no record of a drastic change from sinner to saint.

Truth is, we strayed whenever our focus on anything or anyone (including self) replaced our focus on God. Folks within the church still need the saving grace of Jesus Christ to rescue us from self-righteous attitudes, prejudices, and bad habits. We may even have come to our senior years, comparing ourselves with others. But beyond attendance and abstinence, God sees our heart with all its iniquities, which we try so hard to hide.

The good news is that God searches for church members with the same urgency and passion as He searches for non-members. He knows that always being present is different from being faithful. He knows when testimonies about His goodness are tinted with doubt. He knows when we're lost and are afraid to admit it. In His love, He searches for us to replace our fake goodness with His perfect righteousness, made possible only by the sacrificial death of Christ.

Now, get personal. Think how God rejoices when you accept His love as the only source of our salvation! You're not just a number in the flock. You're the heart He yearns to reach, when your fellowship with Him just takes you through the motions. You're the one He lifts onto His shoulders and carries through the darkness, when you're too drowsy to see clearly. You will never feel lost if you keep the vision of your loving, lifting Fatherly Shepherd in your mind. Let it inspire your wholehearted devotion.

PRAYER: Heavenly Shepherd, thank You for loving us and searching for us, even when we do not acknowledge that we have strayed. Thanks for lifting us onto Your shoulder and bringing us home. In Jesus' name, Amen.

This Week's Prayer Guide

Sunday
"When God forgives, He at once restores." (Theodore Epp)

Monday
Here you are, in your later years, understanding and appreciating how for your entire life, the Good Shepherd has been loving and seeking after you. Thank Him for His grace (more kindness than you deserve), and His mercy (less penalty than you deserve).

Tuesday
Does your awareness of God's mercy keep you from judging other people who stray? Pray that you demonstrate

God's love, grace, and mercy in the way you relate to both Christians and non-Christians.

Wednesday
It's difficult for struggling Christians to relate to you, if you make it appear that you were always strong. Pray to mention your weakness, if only for the purpose of emphasizing God's forgiveness, and encouraging the listener to rely on God's strength.

Thursday
Imagine yourself as the sheep on God's shoulder. Pray that it will encourage you, whenever you begin to feel discouraged or worthless.

Friday
Here is my favorite verse from Elizabeth Cecilia Clephane's song "There Were Ninety and Nine." Sing or meditate:

> Lord, thou hast here thy ninety and nine;
> are they not enough for thee?
> But the Shepherd made answer:
> "This of mine has wandered away from me,
> and although the road be rough and steep,
> I go to the desert to find my sheep."

Saturday
Thank God for searching, finding, and restoring you. Help in the restoration of others who were lost, but now are found, and need a human voice or touch to encourage them.

CUPFUL #50

SABBATH REST

> Then Jesus said to the Pharisees, "The Sabbath day was made to help people. People were not made to be ruled by the Sabbath."
>
> (MARK 2:27)

My friend relocated from the Virgin Islands to Texas for a job assignment. Those were the days before GPS or MapQuest©, so he bought an old-fashioned map. All went well, until the day he tried to drive home without using it.

He drove for an hour before admitting to himself that he was lost. He stopped at a gas station, took out his map, and asked the attendant, "Could you please show me where I am on this map?" The attendant informed him, "You're off the map." He had driven outside the region the map covered, and he was fully responsible for his plight.

The Sabbath is the weekly attendant that God put in place to help us stay within healthy bounds of our ADLs (activities of daily living). Our Creator loves us. He requires that after the first six days of hectic toil, we rest. Resting from life's hustle and bustle on the last day of the week, is God's plan to revive not only our bodies but also our minds. When we neglect Sabbath rest, we tend to overwork, and extend ourselves off the map of reasonable living.

The command in Exodus 20:8-11 requires that our entire household adhere to that rest, and use the day for worship. After we have worked for the first six days, we put away tools, check books, schedules and anything which interferes with active worship. The Sabbath was made to help us relax, reset and reboot our bodies and brains. It gives us time for fellowship with one another, to help each other grow spiritually.

Aging folks especially need the Sabbath, not to force us into rest, but to secure for us, the rest we need. Our minds rejuvenate when we spend the entire day, focusing positively on God and Heaven! He created the Sabbath for our benefit. Let us enjoy the sacred Sabbath rest which helps us live longer and stronger!

PRAYER: Creator God, thank you for giving us what is best for us, including the Sabbath, in Jesus' name, Amen.

This Week's Prayer Guide

Sunday
"Keeping the Sabbath teaches us to trust God and enjoy Him…It's God's way to set us free from worry and anxiety, ambition and adrenaline, self-importance and anger, even loneliness." (Bill Gaultiere)

Monday
God's instructions were, "Remember the Sabbath day to keep it holy." (Exodus 20:8) Pray for the habit of obedience to remember it. How easy it is for older folks to forget!

Tuesday
The command also informed us that God rested on the first Sabbath day. (Exodus 20:11) He was not tired, because He's

God. Why do you think He rested? Pray for the courage to do as He did.

Wednesday
Pray to have like-minded friends and relatives with whom you can enjoy Sabbath fellowship.

Thursday
Emergency humanitarian help and deeds of kindness are considered good Sabbath activities. Pray for discernment to see opportunities to share compassion on the Sabbath day.

Friday
God so loved the world in general, and you in particular, that not only did He send Jesus to save you, He also made sure that all your needs, including your need for rest is met. Thank Him for being so loving and so wise.

Saturday
O Day of Rest and Gladness by Christopher Wordsworth provides a fitting meditation as we contemplate Sabbath rest.

> "O day of rest and gladness, O day of joy and light,
> O balm of care and sadness, most beautiful, most bright;
> On thee the high and lowly through ages joined in tune,
> Sing 'Holy, holy, holy' to the great God Triune."

CUPFUL #51

CHRISTMAS CELEBRATION

> The Father sent his Son to be the Savior of the world.
> (1 John 4:14)

We did not celebrate Christmas in my childhood home, but an experience in my adult years gave me reason to celebrate God's gift of His Son, every day.

It was around the middle of December and I was broke. I still had not been able to send home the Christmas card with money, which every Caribbean parent expects from a child who lives abroad. I plucked up enough courage to make the call to my mother. She answered promptly and surprised me.

"I'm glad you called," she said as gleefully as I ever heard her. "Remember that lady who borrowed your money and never paid you back?" She mentioned the lady's name and reminded me of an incident that I had long forgotten. "She became a Christian, and she decided to make restitution. She brought all of your money. I'm keeping it for you."

In similar glee, I responded, "You keep it. That will be my Christmas gift to you this year."

The real excitement in this story is that the salvation that came to the world on the first Christmas morning, offers not only salvation from sin—but also the everyday consequences that result from sin. For the lady, it was salvation from a life of callousness and salvation from guilt. For me, it was salvation from embarrassment. For my mother, it was salvation from disappointment. Have you ever stopped to count the many undesirable incidents and emotions we are spared every day, only because Christ came?

There was so much to celebrate that first Christmas. Love, joy, peace, and goodwill have been added to our lives through God's gift of His Son, Jesus Christ. Celebrate this gift every day!

PRAYER: Thank You, God, that along with Your gift of forgiveness when we repent from our sins, we have access to a better life on earth, and the prospect of the best life You have reserved for us, when You return as King. In Jesus' name, Amen

This Week's Prayer Guide

Sunday
"You can never truly enjoy Christmas until you can look up into the Father's face and tell him you have received His Christmas gift." (John R. Rice)

Monday
Thank God that the greatest Christmas gift, Jesus Christ, also called Immanuel (God with us), is available to you, and to everyone else.

Tuesday
What gift will you give to Christ, to celebrate His birth? Pray that your entire life will be your gift, surrendered completely to Him.

Wednesday
Attributed to John Francis Wade, "O Come All Ye Faithful is a popular Christmas Carol that calls people together to honor Christ.

> O come, all ye faithful, joyful and triumphant,
> O come ye, O come ye to Bethlehem.
> Come and behold him, born the king of angels.
>
> Refrain:
> O come let us adore him, O come let us adore him,
> O come let us adore him, Christ the Lord.
>
> Yea, Lord, we greet thee, born this happy morning,
> Jesus, to thee be all glory giv'n;
> Word of the Father, now in flesh appearing.

Thursday
Pray to honor Christ in every part of your Christmas celebration. Eat healthfully and temperately. Include Him in your conversation.

Friday
Pray for opportunity to share His love while you share other gifts with your loved ones.

Saturday
Pray for the desire to celebrate Jesus, not annually, but daily.

CUPFUL #52

RESERVED BLESSINGS

> The Lord blessed Job with even more
> than he had in the beginning.
>
> (Job 42:12)

The story of Job begins with an excellent description of his spirituality, his social status, and his wealth. "He was a good, honest man. He respected God and refused to do evil. Job had seven sons and three daughters … He had many servants. He was the richest man in the east" (Job 1:1–3). The story also ends with an excellent conclusion. "Job lived to be a very old man who had lived a good, long life" (Job 42:17).

But between the beginning and the ending, Job's life took a deep, dark detour. He lost all his children, his servants, and his possessions. His body became ravaged with painful sores. His wife discouraged him, and his friends misjudged him. He seemed sentenced to a life of misery and suffering, but that was not the destination God planned for him. God held his blessings in reserve.

In the midst of life's hardships, when the enemy of our souls tries to convince us that we are disadvantaged and defeated, Jesus offers us the power and strength to remain faithful. "Even if I walk through a valley as dark as the grave," the psalmist affirms, "I will not be afraid of any danger, because you are with me" (Psalm 23:4). God stays with us in our pain and difficulties, and He does not abandon His original plan for us to live saved and satisfied.

Even if struggles and disappointments have occupied most of your years, they do not decide how your life will end. Whenever you begin to feel hopeless, remember how in Job's later years, God gave Him access to his reserved blessings. God may surprise you in the same way. He can give you your blessings now, in a few years, or even later, in the new earth. Remain purposeful, faithful, hopeful, and loving! Yes, you can, through Christ who gives you the strength!

PRAYER: Dear God, we thank You for always being with us, and for the blessings you have planned for us. In Jesus' name, Amen.

This Week's Prayer Guide

Sunday
"Gratitude lifts our eyes off the things we lack so we might see the blessings we possess." (Max Lucado)

Monday
What valuables have you lost within the last year? What valuables do you have left? Pray a prayer of gratitude to God, that along with all your other blessings, you have life.

Tuesday
Thank God that despite the detours, God was always with you, and you are still on the road to your destination of eternal life.

Wednesday
Thank God for enjoyable fellowship with friends along the way.

Thursday
Pray today for specific persons who are still on the wrong path, that they might follow God back to the right path.

Friday
Here are two verses from "Count Your Blessings," written by Johnson Oatman Jr. They help us enjoy the journey.

> When upon life's billows you are tempest-tossed,
> When you are discouraged, thinking all is lost,
> Count your many blessings; name them one by one,
> And it will surprise you what the Lord has done.
> Chorus:
> Count your blessings; name them one by one.
> Count your blessings; see what God hath done.
>
> So amid the conflict, whether great or small,
> Do not be discouraged; God is over all.
> Count your many blessings; angels will attend,
> Help and comfort give you to your journey's end.

Saturday
Pray to remain faithful from now until you see Jesus face to face.

Fruitfulness in Old Age

Good people are like budding palm trees.
They grow strong like the cedar trees of Lebanon.
They are planted in the house of the Lord.

They grow strong there in the courtyards of our God.
Even when they are old,
They will continue producing fruit like young, healthy trees.
They are there to show everyone that the Lord is good.

He is my Rock, and he does no wrong.
                        Psalm 92:12–15

TEACH Services, Inc.
P U B L I S H I N G

We invite you to view the complete
selection of titles we publish at:
www.TEACHServices.com

We encourage you to write us
with your thoughts about this,
or any other book we publish at:
info@TEACHServices.com

TEACH Services' titles may be purchased in
bulk quantities for educational, fund-raising,
business, or promotional use.
bulksales@TEACHServices.com

Finally, if you are interested in seeing
your own book in print, please contact us at:
publishing@TEACHServices.com
We are happy to review your manuscript at no charge.

www.ingramcontent.com/pod-product-compliance
Lightning Source LLC
Chambersburg PA
CBHW070551160426
43199CB00014B/2464